NAZARÉ
*Women and Men in a Prebureaucratic Portuguese
Fishing Village*

NAZARÉ

WOMEN AND MEN IN A PREBUREAUCRATIC PORTUGUESE FISHING VILLAGE

JAN BRØGGER

University of Trondheim, Norway

Harcourt Brace Jovanovich College Publishers

Fort Worth   Philadelphia   San Diego   New York   Orlando   Austin   San Antonio
Toronto   Montreal   London   Sydney   Tokyo

Publisher	Ted Buchholz
Acquisitions Editor	Christopher Klein
Project Editor	Mike Hinshaw
Production Manager	Thomas Urquhart
Manager of Art & Design	Guy Jacobs
Cover Design	Guy Jacobs

Library of Congress Cataloging-in-Publication Data

Brøgger, Jan.
    Nazaré : women and men in a prebureaucratic Portuguese fishing
village / Jan Brøgger.
        p.   cm. — (Case studies in cultural anthropology)
    Includes bibliographical references.
    ISBN 0-03-043382-7
    1. Nazaré (Portugal)—Social conditions.   2. Social structure-
-Portugal—Nazaré.   3. Sex role—Portugal—Nazaré.   4. Women-
-Portugal—Nazaré—Social conditions.   5. Fishers—Portugal—Nazaré-
-Social conditions.   I. Title.   II. Series.
    HN600.N39B76   1992
    305.3'09469'42—dc20   91-32074
                                                                                      CIP

Address for editorial correspondence:
Harcourt Brace Jovanovich, Publishers; 301 Commerce Street; Suite 3700; Fort Worth, TX 76102

Address for orders:
Harcourt Brace Jovanovich, Publishers; 6277 Sea Harbor Drive; Orlando, FL 32887 1-800-782-
4479, or 1-800-433-0001 (in Florida)

Printed in the United States of America

2 3 4 5 016 9 8 7 6 5 4 3 2 1

Foreword

ABOUT THE SERIES

These case studies in cultural anthropology are designed for students in beginning and intermediate courses in the social sciences, to bring them insights into the richness and complexity of human life as it is lived in different ways, in different places. The authors are men and women who have lived in the societies they write about and who are professionally trained as observers and interpreters of human behavior. Also, the authors are teachers—in their writing, the needs of the student reader remain foremost. It is our belief that when an understanding of ways of life very different from one's own is gained, abstractions and generalizations about the human condition become meaningful.

The scope and character of the series has changed continually since we published the first case studies in 1960. We are concerned with ways in which human groups and communities are coping with the massive changes wrought in their physical and social environments during recent decades. We are also concerned with the ways in which established cultures have met life's problems. And we want to include representation of the various modes of communication and emphasis that are being formed and reformed as anthropology itself changes.

We think of the Case Studies in Cultural Anthropology as an instructional series, intended for use in the classroom. We have always used case studies in our teaching, whether for neophytes or advanced graduate students. We start with case studies, whether from our own series or from elsehwere, and weave our way into theory, and then return to cases. For us, they are the grounding of our discipline.

ABOUT THE AUTHOR

Jan Brøgger, born in Paris in 1936, is the son of a Norwegian writer and journalist. He embarked on a career as a psychologist with a psychoanalytical orientation. In 1964 he was invited to the Department of Psychology at Cornell University, Ithaca, N.Y. Inspired by Victor V. Turner and John M. Roberts, then at Cornell, he changed his field to social anthropology, returning to Norway in 1965 to study with Fredrik Barth in Bergen. His first fieldwork among peasants in southern Italy confirmed his strong interest in the Catholic European south. He received his Ph.D. in Oslo in 1970, and worked for five years as a senior curator at the University Ethnographic Museum there.

From 1970 to 1971 he did fieldwork among the Sidamo of southwestern Ethiopia, but returned on his subsequent fieldwork to the European south, this time to Portugal, where he has, apart from some applied anthropology in Sudan, for the past 12 years concentrated his studies, developing a historical anthropology with the object of understanding the prebureaucratic style of life that prevailed in Europe before the industrial revolution. He has also studied the Portuguese-speaking descendants of the ancient conquerors of Malacca in Malaysia.

Brøgger has since 1975 held a chair of social anthropology at the University of Trondheim, Norway. In 1985 he was chosen as the first Special European Awardee in Anthropology by the Association for Anthropological Diplomacy, Politics, and Society. He has published several anthropological monographs.

In Norway, Brøgger is also known as a political commentator, and is a columnist in Norway's largest serious newspaper, *Aftenposten,* in Oslo. He has written several books on the nature of totalitarianism and is director of the independent Liberal Research Institute in Oslo.

He is married and has six children.

ABOUT THIS CASE STUDY

This remarkable study of Nazaré, a Portuguese fishing community, is much more than an ethnography of a small, "traditional" village. It is an analysis of styles of social relationship that appear to have been in force in greater Europe before the rise of capitalism and industrial "civilization"—a prebureaucratic style. This style has consequences for a large range of social relations but also for personal development. In Nazaré, the intimate dyadic relationships, as in the companionate marriage of the contemporary West, are not available. People are socialized within a communal framework that lacks theme. The concepts of personhood, and of self, in Nazaré are therefore quite different than in contemporary European society, more representative of *l'ancien régime* of the medieval world before the Reformation.

This analysis is placed between the rural–urban models of society. In the European tradition, the former is communal and "sacred" and the latter is differentiated and "profane." The former is what American anthropologists have more often termed the "folk" society, in relation to which "urban" society can be seen as a kind of antithesis.

This is a case study of a community where individuation and privatization have not assumed their modern, *bourgeois* form. For this reason it is somehow familiar, since this is also true of most communities anthropologists have studied in depth, but surprising, even shocking at times, because Nazaré is a European community, in but not of the twentieth century.

Nazaré is also a community where women rule the home and the street and where men and women prefer the company of their own gender mates rather than the companionship of the conjugal relationship. Men are not welcome around the house after a perfunctory breakfast. They spend their time either at one of the *tabernas,* on the beach preparing for fishing, or out on the water in one of several kinds of fishing boats. The household is matrifocal, and the temper of the household is also that of the community. Women speak out, they speak up, and men take a "back seat"—even to the point of looking mild and somewhat withdrawn. Nazaré is one of the most clearcut cases of female dominance in and beyond the home in the anthropological literature, and one of the reasons for this is that dichotomy of private and public responsible for so much of gender-linked role allocation is not developed in this community.

This case study is, in its style, foci, and points of reference, somewhat different than most of the studies in our series. We have, partly for this reason, found it stimulating, informative, and fun, and we hope that our readers find it so also. It is worth a careful and thoughtful reading.

George and Louise Spindler
Series Editors
Ethnographics, P. O. Box 38
Calistoga, CA 94515

Acknowledgments

The research on which this monograph is based was supported by The Norwegian Research Council for Sciences and the Humanities, Oslo, Wenner-Gren Foundation for Anthropological Research, New York and Fundacão Calouste Gulbenkian, Lisboa.

A number of Nazarenos of all ages, men and women, boys and girls, have contributed to this study. First of all my assistant and collaborator for many years José Maria dos Santos Trindade and in alphabetic order: António Balau, Orlando Escorrega, Maria Cândida Galego, Isidro Carlinhos Meca, Lisete Galego Ricardo Trindade, António Sarieira and João Paulo Ova Robalo.

The chapters developed from seminars at the Department of Social Anthropology in Trondheim, and I wish to thank Harald Aspen, Carla Dahl-Jørgensen, Bjørn B. Erring, Stein E. Johansen and Eli Am for stimulating discussion and criticism. I am also indebted to George and Louise Spindler and Steven Borish for criticism and encouragement and to Dag Sagafoss for drawings and diagrams. Finally I wish to thank my wife Bodil Brøgger for her unfailing support and interest.

Jan Brøgger
Trondheim, Norway

Contents

1 / Preparing for Fieldwork

When I was preparing for my first fieldwork it was clear to me that I had to present my choice in strictly scientific terms. I was offered the possibility of going to Southern Sudan, to classical anthropological territory, so to speak. But I had actually fallen in love with the Mediterranean, and had a difficult time explaining in scientific terms why I really thought Italy was a better choice. As a matter of fact, I did not succeed. My instructor, Fredrik Barth, did not take my theoretical apology for the anthropological legitimacy of Italian peasants at face value. But he understood and even accepted my real and highly personal motivation: a deep fascination with the neo-Latin peoples of Southern Europe that, paraphrasing Edward W. Said (1959), may be referred to as Mediterraneanism.

Said demonstrated how a similar fascination with the near Orient has been created by the joint forces of poets, novelists, historians, travellers and others who have created a mystique that gives a particular structure to the Western perception of the Near East. Psychologically this mystique is related to patriotism and other emotionally charged ideas about territories and people, ideas that reach beyond the objective world of positive science and into the field of humanistic sentiment that traditionally has been left to the arts. With the coming of age of the social sciences however, its practitioners are more aware of social reality as a created phenomenon. Following the work of Erving Goffman (1959) and Berger and Luckmann (1966), among others, social scientists know what the writer Ibsen told his audience more than a century ago: social reality is a construction that sometimes approaches illusion. Our perception of cultures has much in common with our perception of people. We hardly notice the shortcomings of the persons we love and care for. In fact, we fail to notice the imperfections that are a part of the human condition. That is what real love is all about, as pointed out by the Norwegian philosopher Ingjald Nissen, who maintains that "love between human beings is in large measure dependent upon the fact that one person overlooks and covers up the shortcomings of the other. It is one of the most beautiful phenomena in social life that shortcomings which are not acknowledged lose their realness." This also holds for cultures.

For example, I know that many travellers have failed to recognize the charm of Naples. Some of them have seen nothing but filth and poverty, which of course is also a part of the scenery. I am unable to prove that my perception of the Mediterranean and its people is true in any objective sense of the word. It is all a question of meaning, and what we may aspire to understand is how meaning is created in human societies. That is at least one of the main tasks of social anthropology. What I have referred to as Mediterraneanism is the complex of ideas and sentiments that generations of humanists, philosophers, writers, historians, and travellers have created through their various presentations of the Mediterranean world. Much of our European identity is associated with the Mediterranean—as the center of the Roman Empire, and later of the Roman Catholic Church. On the Mediterranean stage were presented some of the most impressive shows of Renaissance art and intellectualism. Its magnificent ruins are also part of the intricate pattern of meaning that fosters the irresistible fascination of Mediterraneanism. I suspect that quite a few anthropologists share a similar fascination for other parts of the world, and that this fascination may be an essential part of the anthropological search for understanding. At any rate it has been a major force behind my involvement with the Mediterranean during the past three decades.

My first fieldwork was carried out in a peasant village in Calabria in Southern Italy (Brøgger 1971). During this fieldwork I became even more addicted to the Mediterranean mystique. However, the fascination gradually matured into a more goal-directed search for meaning. It is in my case an empirical fact that the association with Mediterranean people opened a new and extremely rewarding world of social relationships. The Mediterranean people are in a number of ways different from northern Europeans, yet we share with them cultural ideas as members of Christian civilization. One of the most important differences, in historical terms, is undoubtedly that northern Europe was subjected to the shattering cultural revolution known as the Protestant Reformation. Through the Protestant Reformation, puritanism became a dominant theme in the northerners' state of being, changing people from comparatively obedient servants of tradition into hard workers in search of progress, perfection, and individual achievement. The northerners became the first champions of industrialism while the southerners remained for several centuries more or less traditional agriculturalists.

Pockets of preindustrial societies today remain at the margins of the Mediterranean world. The importance of these societies for anthropological understanding is obvious. In certain respects they represent the point of departure for the cultural changes that Karl Polanyi (1944) has referred to as *The Great Transformation*. In human cultural history, the changes from *l'ancien régime* of the preindustrial world to modern times of industry and science will probably be regarded at least as momentous as the neolithic revolution. The human condition has been radically changed, not only with regard to easily observed systems of production and distribution, but also with regard to the less obvious patterns of social relationships, thought, and consciousness. These parameters of development were the concern of late nineteenth-century sociologists. Ferdinand Tönnies in Germany and Emil Durkheim in France both made the same observation that in modern times a new form of society emerged that radically changed the nature of social relationships. In the preindustrial village most of the necessities of life are negotiated through face-to-face relationships in closed and many-stranded networks. Villagers "inherit" their social networks, so to speak, and are forced to collaborate in a number of respects. They are for better or worse dependent upon each other. Athough they are not exposed to the alienation of city life, they have to rub shoulders with kith, kin, and neighbors while having few possibilities for individual management of their lives. Tønnies referred to this order as a *Gemeinschaft*. The most outstanding feature of the Gemeinschaft-village is its *communality*. Private life scarcely exists and the villagers spend their time *together* whether in work or in leisure. But the community is split into two gender cultures. Even after marriage the spouses continue to spend most of their time in the company of their respective gender groups.

In an industrial community the market is the crucial institution. When the necessities of life in the broadest possible sense are negotiated through an impersonal market rather than through personal face-to-face exchanges, people become less dependent upon each other. They gain individual freedom, but at the cost of the tight social network of the Gemeinschaft. Their networks are created and based on contracts and therefore are less stable and not restricted to the narrow confines of a local community. The dyadic relationship, a more or less exclusive relationship between two people, gains in importance at the cost of the communality. A community in which relationships of this order prevail, Tønnies referred to as a *Gesellschaft*. However, this text refers to the Gesellschaft with the more familiar term **urban society** and to the Gemeinschaft with the term **folk community.** Although the folk communities in the United States have a somewhat different historical background than do the traditional villages in Europe, they share a number of characteristics, the most essential of which is the egalitarian and close-knit nature of social relationships sustained by tradition within the framework of a rural economy.

The traditional rural communities, to the degree that they still exist, offer an opportunity to explore the everyday life that elsewhere has been transformed by urbanization. But they are important also from another point of view. Historians such as Emmanuel Le Roy Ladurie (1978), Lawrence Stone (1977), Philippe Ariès (1960), and Edward Shorter (1975) have on the basis of historical documents presented crucial information on village life, family systems, and childhood in former times. Given the historical perspective, trends sometimes emerge that a contemporary could not have understood. With a focus on everyday life of bygone days in Europe, scholars have created a new discipline that Peter Burke (1987) has referred to as historical anthropology. Again to the degree that contemporary societies in Europe have preserved as survivals elements of a preindustrial past, the field anthropologist may join forces with the historical anthropologist in the description and understanding of preindustrial Europe and The Great Transformation. A historical perspective therefore is not merely legitimate, but essential. It gives meaning to social forms and elements of behavior that, seen outside a historical context, would remain hidden.

With these ideas in mind I decided to do my third fieldwork in the most traditional (except for the then inaccessible Rumania) of the neo-Latin countries: Portugal. In order to make the best choice of a local community for participant observation, I made an extensive tour of Portugal with my nine-year-old daughter in the spring of 1978. Starting in Lisbon we went south toward the Algarve coast, visiting many villages along the way. In Alentejo we observed collective farms, transformed from landed estates in the wake of the revolution of 1974 when a communist-inspired military government had decided to implement socialism. Further south we encountered villages partly depopulated by emigration, and along the Algarve coast we observed villages that had changed from traditional communities into service-centers for tourism. We saw high-rise buildings and villas with swimming-pools populated by northern Europeans in pursuit of the sun. Although we observed a rather fascinating melange of traditional and modern forms of living, I concluded that, as far as these territories were concerned, we were too late. Only a passionate student in social change would confidently choose a site in this area.

More promising was our excursion to the northern parts of the country. Particularly in the Tras os Montes we encountered truly traditional communities with very few signs of progress and modernization. Without exception they were victims of a mass exodus of the younger men. Leaving their wives, children, and parents behind, the young and able-bodied men had moved to establish themselves as guest-workers in France, Switzerland, Germany, and England. Although of great theoretical interest, these partly depopulated villages were not what we were looking for. In a somewhat discouraged frame of mind we reached the coast of central Portugal. To find a comparatively intact rural village of the kind found in Southern Italy in the middle of the 1960s (Brøgger 1971) was apparently more than we could hope for in Portugal at the end of the 1970s. At that time I felt a certain nostalgia and also a sting of envy, thinking of the preceding generation of anthropologists who had so much virgin anthropological territory at their disposal: Pitt-Rivers' pre-industrial Spain, Goodenough's and Spiro's Micronesia, not to mention Malinowski's Trobrianders, or Fortes' Tallensi's, and Boas' Kwakiutl.

As we approached the waterfront I spotted a high-rise building of the kind that has transformed the beaches of Algarve into the urbanized vacation landscape that is the hallmark of twentieth-century mass-tourism, an ominous sign indeed. As we came closer, we discovered that it was a lone monster overlooking a village of whitewashed buildings of humane proportions. We had reached Nazaré, one of the main centers of fishing along the Atlantic coast of Portugal. We entered the village along the main street skirting one of the most magnificent beaches in Europe. In strange contrast to the multitude of desolate villages we had visited, this one was teeming with life. Women, who obviously were not tourists, moved along the shore in both directions in busy pursuit of important undertakings, judging from the rhythm of their gait and the expression of determination on their faces. On the beach were gathered a polychromatic assortment of fishing-vessels. Obviously they had been pulled onto the sandy beach because of the lack of a proper harbor or lagoon. Surrounding the vessels was a crowd of men busily mending their nets. The women were not dressed up according to cosmopolitan European standards but wore outfits that gave us the impression of being national costumes. Several of the men wore long black caps.

Our tourist guide, a somewhat embarrassing necessity for a self-respecting anthropologist, confirmed this impression. The fishing village of Nazaré is famous for its folklore and scenic beauty. In less than an hour after our arrival we had decided that our first goal had been achieved. We had found what we were looking for: an authentic local community that, judging from the appearance and demeanor of its population, had not sold out to modern times.

ENCOUNTERING NAZARÉ

Compared to the historical arrival of Raymond Firth in Tikopia and Evans-Pritchard in the Nuer, our arrival in Nazaré four months later was a true non-event. No awestricken or unfriendly natives gathered round. We were not even, as Clifford Geertz on Bali, overlooked. We simply drowned in the mass of visitors. August is the holiday month *par excellence* in continental Europe, and Nazaré was at our arrival filled with tourists, both Portuguese and foreign. We had, however, no problems arranging accommodation. During the holiday season all authentic Nazarenos move from their homes to primitive housing in order to get a stake in the tourist trade. All sorts of accommodations are available, from luxury-apartments to plain rooms with the barest necessities. We settled for a decent, average apartment in the northern part of the town. We had some rather tough negotiations with the landlady. Although illiterate, she was a formidable woman who had succeeded in establishing herself as a prosperous businesswoman. She was hard-headed and not visibly eager to please, and she knew exactly what she wanted. Her husband appeared rather meek in comparison. He was running a restaurant under the protection of his wife. As we were to find out later, he was one of the few fishermen who had succeeded in establishing himself in a bourgeois trade. As such he was exceptional. In other ways, however, he was typical of the Nazareno male, particularly with regard to his wife, who was the obvious head of the household.

When moving into the apartment with my wife and six children from the ages 4 to 16, we must have seemed like run of the mill tourists. The only exception was the composition of our family, consisting of one pair of twins and one pair of triplets with a nine-year-old girl in between the litters, so to speak: five girls and one boy. As I was to learn later, this was, with regard to gender, a most fortunate situation from the local point of view.

Given my passion for traditional Mediterranean villages, I had during the first couple of weeks grave doubts about the wisdom of my choice of community. However, I took some comforts from my previous fieldwork experiences in Italy and Africa, which had both started with similar feelings of uncertainty. But this time the doubts seemed better founded. Because I had no intention of studying mass-tourism, what could I possibly get from the present confusion? The beach, which during my first visit was dominated by the picturesque assortment of fishing vessels, was now completely settled with neat rows of tents, conjuring up images of a Turkish military camp from the last century. Under the tents languished a crowd of sunbathing tourists in swimsuits. Every little street was filled with people going to and from the beach. The local people who had impressed my daughter and me during our first visit were almost unnoticeable amidst the mass of visitors.

After getting the practical matters settled, my wife and I spent hours discussing our predicament. Given my interest in the traditional Mediterranean world, had we made a serious mistake settling in one of the favorite tourist spots in Portugal? As usual, my wife was full of encouragement and reminded me of my initial despair during our first weeks in Calabria, which proved to be completely unfounded. She insisted that in Nazaré—just like in Montevarese—we certainly would discover a different world beneath the immediate surface.

In Italy, and particularly in Africa, there had been few problems getting the fieldwork started. Establishing contact with the local population had been comparatively easy because we were received with curiosity and interest. In Nazaré, however, we had to "share" the local population with a crowd of competitors. And from the local point of view, the anthropologist and his family could hardly be distinguished from the other visitors. This was a somewhat unusual situation for an anthropologist. Without being conscious of the fact, I was struggling with the legacy of colonial anthropology. From its very beginning, anthropology emerged in the wake of European exploration and conquest, which promoted an inequality between the anthropologist and "his" or "her" people. Even in countries that had not been subjected to actual colonization, the anthropologist usually was defined as a person of some power and importance. Whether admitted or not, this "other" or "special" status has probably been a part of the traditional definition of the anthropologist's field situation. Participant observation has therefore probably in most cases been a euphemism for the privileged participation of the resident stranger— and not just any stranger, but a stranger with some prestige and resources. To do fieldwork without the aura of borrowed charisma that most anthropologists in the field have enjoyed in the past is an experience for which few of us are prepared. At least I found it comparatively difficult and rather frustrating to make myself interesting to the Nazarenos, whom I finally located in their special bars, which, even at the height of the tourist season, they try to keep for themselves.

In the territory of the fishermen in the back streets of Nazaré, I was through my appearance alone an obvious intruder. At least I discovered that the local population of fishermen kept a considerable distance from the tourists. I also discovered that they kept at a considerable distance from the Nazaré bourgeoisie. An almost caste-like chasm divided the fishermen and the outsiders. In addition to the problems of identity, I also faced a language barrier. Although I mastered a measure of Linguaphone Portuguese, it was, at first, sorrowfully insufficient for meaningful conversation with the local fishermen of Nazaré. Sentences like "My son is playing beneath the grand piano" could hardly be adapted to the situation. However, I gradually discovered the unwritten rules through which my Italian could be converted into a comparatively intelligible Portuguese. The language problem therefore was less formidable than finding a meaningful identity of legitimacy and interest to the local population. Not that I was treated unkindly in any way. My questions were answered politely enough, but after an embarrassingly short period of time, my friendly natives got bored with me. It takes an incredible stamina and self-confidence to impose a presence under these conditions.

Somewhat shamefully I discovered that I was deficient in these qualities, finding it all too easy to avoid the ordeal of the fishermen's *tabernas*. Somehow I came to accept the role that was imposed on me: the resident tourist. I strolled up and down the magnificent beach, stopping for an occasional drink at the sidewalk cafès, observing at a distance groups of fishermen mending their nets. I simply could not summon the courage to approach them, and I still believe I was well advised not to. If the *taberna* was a somewhat forbidding place, the beach was even more so. For a tourist to approach these working men on the main scene of the town would have been a tactless intrusion indeed. The situation was not staged for

The cobblestoned back streets of Nazaré are scenic and give you a feeling of intimacy.

contact. The world of the tourist and the world of the fishermen did not intersect, and indeed were not supposed to.

It suddenly dawned on me that the prevalence of the national costume in Nazaré had something to do with the matter. The costumes were indeed an ethnic uniform that helped to define the identity of the local population in the face of the enormous influx of visitors. It also occurred to me that the problems of establishing rapport with the stratum of fishermen should not be recorded as a personal failure, but as data. What I realized was that among the fishermen, it was not regarded as proper to associate on equal terms either with the tourists or with the local bourgeoisie. As I was to discover later, a fisherman who became too friendly with an outsider of these categories would be criticized, and sometimes accused of being an *engraixador,* that is, someone who seeks favors from people of resources through charm and fictitious friendship. The distance was kept as a protection of the local culture.

My wife had no easier time in trying to establish rapport with the female gender-culture of Nazaré. The women of Nazaré were vastly different from the friends she had in Italy, and her experience with female gender-culture both abroad and back home did not help much, either. The Nazarenas presented themselves as dominating personalities, speaking with loud, somewhat masculine voices. They were busy most of the time with their various schemes, which included managing the businesses of their families. The women did not congregate in the bars. Their homes were their main arenas of meeting, apart from the river where they washed their laundry. Like their menfolk, they were not particularly interested in contact with outsiders. It was an oddly comforting fact that both my wife and I shared the experience of being rejected by the local population.

Our children met with fewer problems. The older girls soon got involved with the children of the bourgeoisie, some of whom would later be their companions at the private high school in Nazaré. The younger children were easily accepted by their age-mates, who did not share the reserve of their elders in the face of resident tourists.

As the tourists gradually left, the local population reemerged like rocks at low tide. The atmosphere changed and we became more visible, and to a certain degree, more interesting. However, it was difficult to shed the stigma of belonging to a class from which the fishermen customarily kept some distance. My situation changed radically for better when a young man who had almost completed high school approached me as I was walking up and down the *esplanade* along the beach. Although his father was a mechanic, his mother was selling fish and definitely belonged to the stratum of Nazareno fishermen. This young man was interested in writing and journalism. He became my first friend among the local population, and through him, I started my fieldwork proper.

Later it occurred to me that he was one of the few people with whom I managed to sustain a dyadic relationship in Nazaré. This simple fact indicated that he was in the process of alienating himself from the stratum of fishermen. In fact he was an aspiring bourgeois. That was the main reason why he had found me interesting. He introduced me to his circle of friends and acquaintances. Of particular interest was the meeting with a young mason, the son of a fisherman with a large kinship network among the fishermen. He had strong intellectual interests. Eventually he left his job as a mason and started to work full time as my assistant. The meeting with this recently married young man represented a breakthrough in my field efforts. This breakthrough happened after several months of lone struggle that sometimes drove me desperate.

My final victory, however, was gained one evening one of our more distant neighbors, whom I knew superficially through his sons, had bought a new car, which in Nazaré is an extraordinary event that calls for particular celebrations. My neighbor was already halfway through his celebrations, and in an animated mood, when he met me. He invited me to participate, and through my drinking skills I became for the first time part of a group of authentic fishermen. It belongs to the story that he was one of the most successful fishermen in Nazaré. He was, according to local standards, a rich man who could not be suspected of ingratiating himself with the bourgeoisie for economic reasons. As soon as I was accepted by this formidable wizard of a fisherman, the ice was broken. Before long I was enmeshed in a substantial network of friends and comrades. I also became a temporary member of his crew. My participation as a crew member was probably essential to my acceptance as a resident stranger, though I was always referred to as Senhor João, and was unable to completely shed the trappings of my initial status. However, I felt that I had achieved something when a fisherman pointed out that Senhor João should be regarded as my nickname. As is explained later, almost all Nazarenos have nicknames, either inherited or acquired. Most nicknames refer to some peculiarity of their first owners, giving the system of identification a unique personal and unbureaucratic flavor.

When I finally was enmeshed in a network of relationships in Nazaré, I also discovered that I had lost some of my freedom. I somehow belonged to my network and could no longer without great difficulty get involved with people outside it. It was also difficult to sustain a dyadic relationship. People simply were not available for one-on-one encounters, nor did they feel a need for it. Only with my young assistant could a relationship of this type be sustained. However, doing so changed his situation at the same time. As we explored Nazaré together, he became increasingly self-conscious about his own culture and was gradually changed from a full-fledged Nazareno into a fledging anthropologist, who eventually graduated from the University in Lisbon.

I have sometimes wondered if real insight into an alien culture must proceed through a privileged, dyadic relationship. To discuss the more delicate matters of a community, its taboos and idiosyncrasies, requires communicating outside the reach of the collective. This consideration makes it clear how much I owe to my young assistant. Our dialogue during the months of fieldwork was essential to the measure of understanding I achieved regarding Nazaré.

NAZARÉ, HISTORY, AND COMPOSITION

The picturesque village with the biblical sounding name is a comparatively recent settlement on the Atlantic coast 135 kilometers north of Lisbon. Outside its magnificent sweep of sandy beaches is some of the richest fishing in Portugal. Before the beach was settled, these fishing-grounds were exploited by the villages Pederneira and Paredes. Pederneira is Nazaré's next door neighbor. Paredes today is an abandoned village a few kilometers to the north.

The Atlantic coast of Portugal has few natural harbors. Two of these, however, were in former times located in the vicinity of Nazaré. The most important was Pederneira, which today is a landlocked agricultural village. But until the seventeenth century the village was situated by a natural lagoon that opened to the sea a few hundred meters to the south of present day Nazaré. During my fieldwork all that was left of this former access to the sea was a narrow bend of the Alcoa River. Since then a large artificial harbor has been constructed. (This harbor will undoubtedly cause major changes in the life of the Nazaré fishermen. The following discussion is, however, restricted to the pre-harbor Nazaré.)

At the time of my fieldwork the river Alcoa ran along a course that once was the bottom of the lagoon. Pederneira had become landlocked as the sea clogged the exit to the lagoon with sand. In neolithic times the lagoon had been very large, extending inland as far as Maiorga and Alcobaça (consult map on next page). As long as vestiges of the lagoon existed, Pederneira flourished both as a port and a shipbuilding center where several of the great ships of the discoveries of the sea-route to India and of Brazil were constructed. Fishing was probably an activity of negligible importance until the arrival of the settlers from Paredes.

Paredes, also known as Praia da Vitoria, was the second port of importance in the area. But by the end of the fifteenth century this port was blocked by the sand dunes, as was later to happen with the lagoon. The inhabitants of Paredes moved to Pederneira, thus boosting the importance of fishing in this once busy center. Around 1760 these settlers were joined by fishermen from Ilhavo to the north.

The construction of vessels in Nazaré represents an unbroken tradition from the time of the discoveries.

It was in fact the people from Ilhavo who made the first temporary settlements on the beach, which at that time was known as Costa da Senhora da Nazaré. This was an old site, centered on the shrine of the Senhora da Nazaré. For centuries this Virgin was among the most prominent in Portugal, adored by countless pilgrims who ventured to her shrine in Sitio above the beach to plead for help. The image of the Virgin bears its name because legend has it that it was sculpted by St. Joseph himself in Nazareth. Hence the name, and hence the name of the village.

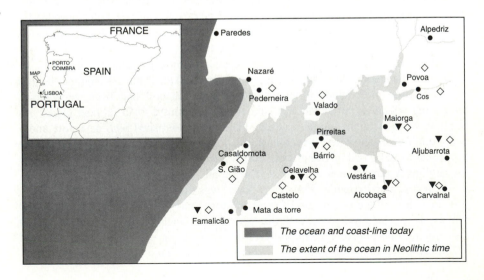

It is known that until 1628 there was not one building of any sort on the beach. During the eighteenth century the fishermen from Ilhavo constructed wooden *cabanas* on the beach and around 1780 about 50 of these cabanas were found there. But mainly because of the pirates, who until the middle of the nineteenth century were preying along the coast, even the fishermen preferred to live in the more protected village of Pederneira when the disappearance of its port made it necessary to keep their boats on the beach. But as soon as the threat of the pirates subsided around the middle of last century, the fishermen descended on the beach and made their permanent homes near the shore (Fonseca 1979).

About the same time the Nazaré beach was discovered by the better-off bourgeoisie of the towns of the interior, thus forecasting the development of tourism. The beach became known as *Praia des banhos* (Bathing beach), and offered the locals an additional source of income. In tune with the spirit of romanticism that prevailed in Europe at that time, the unspoilt or authentic qualities of the life of the fishermen were also appreciated. The fishermen were regarded as living specimens of the noble savage who had perished with the rise of urban civilization elsewhere. The large number of fishermen who congregated on the beach of Nazaré with their decorated boats and typical apparel therefore added to the attraction of the magnificent expanse of fine-grained sand.

Although fishing is regarded as the *raison d'être* of the village, tourism has almost from the beginning of the settlement on *Praia da Nossa Senhora da Nazaré* been part of the economic life of the local population. The fishing population,

The fishermen who congregate on the beach of Nazaré with their decorated boats and typical apparel still have a strong appeal to the romantic idea of folk culture that prevails in the European middle class, and are a treat to urban tourists.

however, did not have the resources nor the expertise to fully exploit the possibilities of tourism. The better part of the income from tourism went to more professional developers who in the latter half of the nineteenth century descended on Nazaré with their projects. Nazaré became for a period a Klondike of construction: during four months in 1875 more than 20 buildings for tourists were constructed (Fonseca 1979). Some of the more successful fishermen no doubt participated in this boom, but the majority of projects were sponsored by what we commonly refer to as representatives of the bourgeois class from Pederneira and beyond.

The tourist industry facilitated the development of two distinct strata in Nazaré, the bourgeoisie and the fishermen, or as the local dialect has it, *pé calçado* (people with shoes) and *gente da praia* (people of the beach). Because the fishermen, *gente da praia,* usually were barefoot, wearing shoes became a critical sign of bourgeois status. The division of the community into two almost caste-like strata is an important factor to consider when approaching the unique culture of the fishermen of Nazaré. The division of the population into two distinct strata is not reflected in the distribution of houses, however. Although the two groups live side by side in the same streets, they manage to avoid each other almost completely.

The layout and style of the architecture adds to the authentic quality of the place and creates a fascinating habitat of narrow streets and whitewashed buildings. Several types of structures can be distinguished.

The public buildings, housing the port administration, the postal services, etc., are all of the same kind with no particularly local characteristics. The same holds for apartment-buildings, whether they were built at the turn of the century or in the 1970s.

The homes of fishermen, however, are of a typically local pattern and are not the product of the cosmopolitan structures in which the traditions and frills of the various academies of architecture are on display. The traditional fishermen houses are built by local artisans from stone and cement, and have the somewhat rustic character found all over the non-urban Mediterranean. Usually they consist of two stories, with a kitchen and a bedroom downstairs and a similar arrangement upstairs.

In addition to these are the so-called *cabanas:* cheap one-storied wooden buildings primarily constructed to accommodate fishing gear and house the families of fishermen during the summer. A few villas are found on the outskirts, testifying to the presence of a few well-to-do bourgeois families.

A brief look at the map of Nazaré reveals the characteristic of the medieval layout (consult map on next page). A row of parallel streets perpendicular to the beach runs without interruption the full length of the village. These streets are flanked by almost parallel rows of small houses constructed wall to wall so as to create long segments of uninterrupted buildings. At about its mid-point this complex is traversed by a street, *Rua Subvila*, the main commercial street of the village. This leaves the central part of Nazaré without traverses, except for one narrow path that runs unsystematically between the row of houses where the builders for some reason have left a gap of about 1 meter (consult map on next page).

A cable-tramway connects Nazaré proper with Sitio at the top of the cliff overlooking the beach settlement. Sitio is administratively an integral part of

Nazaré, but does not display the same parallel system of streets. In other respects it is indistinguishable from Nazaré proper. In the more recently settled periphery of the beach settlement, the layout is more conventional. The *Bairro dos Pescadores,* standing out with its neat rows of identical small houses, represents the only example of social building in the village. Next to the *Bairro dos Pescadores* in the southern part of the village is the food-market where rural producers offer their products alongside the local fish-sellers. In the market can be found all sorts of vegetables and fruits as well as meat and fish. In order to procure fresh food for her household, a woman has to visit the market, *Praça,* at least two times a week.

The population of Nazaré was 8,685 in 1970. Since the official census does not provide information on the division of labor, the fishing population must be calculated on the basis of other information. The number registered with *Casa dos Pescadores* in March 1977 were 1,191. This, however, is not the actual number of active fishermen. Many who are registered as fishermen do other kinds of work in certain periods, particularly construction work, and not all fishermen are registered.

In addition to the fishermen who embark from the shores of Nazaré, a number of men are employed by companies dedicated to large scale fishing on the coasts of Africa, Canada, and Norway. In the north the main prey is the cod-fish, from which is produced the highly esteemed dried cod, *bacalhau;* the northern fishermen, known as *bacalhoeiros,* numbered 137 in 1977. On the coasts of Africa are caught a number of different species, and the activities are known by the geographical name *Cabo Branco*. One hundred seventy men were engaged in *Cabo Branco* fishing in 1977.

No clear distinction should be drawn between the fishermen who engage in the operations in the northern and southern waters and those who operate from the shores of the village. A majority of the fishermen have at one period or another been either *bacalhoeiros* or participated in the *Cabo Branco* expeditions. Only a few remain permanently with these ventures. The majority return to the village and establish themselves as local fishermen. Quite often expeditions to foreign waters are made to raise capital to buy a boat in order to start out as an independent fisherman in home waters.

A number of men from Nazaré also seek employment in the merchant marine. It is an opportunity that strongly appeals to the Nazarenos, because the sea is felt to be the only element truly fit for the local men and offers a comparatively high income. Particularly if employment is secured with a foreign company, the income may be substantial. Those who have had the chance to get employment with a Norwegian company can earn salaries many times higher than the fishermen, and become wealthy by local standards. This is probably the reason why many sailors gradually withdraw from the community of fishermen. Because they usually can afford to buy a comparatively costly apartment and maintain a higher standard of living than their former peers, they often become identified with the bourgeois middle class.

The total number of active fishermen, calculated on the basis of individual boats, was 912 in 1975. Considering the average family size of 5.2, according to a census of families, the number of people strictly belonging to the class of fishermen amount to around 6,000. This means that a little less than two-thirds of the population belong to the class of fishermen. The rest of the population, apart from a small number of bureaucrats and professionals, is engaged in some sort of business enterprise mainly catering to the needs of the tourists.

During the summer the village is inundated by visitors, and in the tourist season from June to September approximately 17,000 tourists lodge in the village. Only a fraction of these live in hotels and pensions. The majority live in privately rented rooms and apartments. Tourism obviously is the second industry in Nazaré. Most families of the fishing class rent rooms or apartments to the tourists. If at all possible the family will move to a cheap *cabana* in the periphery of the village, renting out their home in order to boost their income. The amount of money earned during the summer months may sometimes exceed the income from the fishing. The tourist trade, however, does not offer employment possibilities of any importance to the male members from the fishing population. Most of the restaurants prefer to hire employees from the outside, preferably from the rural areas. One of the reasons for this is that the work has little appeal to the Nazarenos. The fishermen are not disposed to venture into land-based kinds of employment. Out of dire need young men may for a period of time work in construction as assistants to masons. But they rarely stay for long. The feeling is that fishing is the only worthwhile kind of employment, a fact that will be considered in a later chapter.

The situation of the women is different. Since they are not engaged in active fishing, they try to exploit the possibilities offered by the tourist industry. Although the majority have to content themselves with cleaning and laundry jobs, apart from renting their own apartments, a few have succeeded in establishing themselves as wealthy entrepreneurs in the tourist industry. They have done so mainly by putting their savings into buildings primarily built to cater to the tourists. Quite a number of houses and apartments in Nazaré are empty during the winter and only come to life with the advent of the tourists. The majority of these are owned by members of the middle class and investors from outside, but a few belong to successful local women from the strata of fishermen.

The marketing of fish is solidly in the hands of the women. They buy fish at the official fish auction and sell it in the rural hinterland of Nazaré. (According to Portuguese law all the fish must be sold through the official auction.) Many of these female fish-sellers, *peixeiras,* become quite wealthy by local standards. In order to succeed as a fish-seller, however, considerable skill and understanding of the market is necessary. Most of the *peixeiras* have inherited their craft from their mothers and started in the trade at an early age. To enter the rank of the *peixeiras,* therefore, is not easy. It is not enough to have an understanding of the business: a network of clients is necessary. The clients are usually loyal to their habitual fish-sellers, who in many cases have served their families for more than one generation. The *peixeiras* are the trendsetters among the women; they are most visible and impressive. They are very self-conscious, as demonstrated by leading members of

The marketing of fish is solidly in the hands of the women. This photograph of the fish auction shows the fish-sellers, peixeiras, *in action.*

this group. Not a single man from the rank of the fishermen is engaged in the marketing business. If a man is observed among the crowd of women at the auctions, he is certainly not from the *praia*.

This is one of the important expressions of the gender-cultures in Nazaré. There is a clearcut division between the tasks appropriate for men and women, respectively. But unlike the situation that traditionally prevails in both the United States and Europe, the women are also in charge of the economy outside the household. Many women among the stratum of fishermen are business-people in the true sense of the word. This unconventional division of roles between men and women makes the situation in Nazaré particularly interesting. As we shall see in the next chapter, the dominant position of women has important consequences for the conjugal relationship and the family structure.

2 / Female Dominance and Family Structure

As was obvious during our first encounter with Nazaré, even a casual observer would be struck by the dominance of women, both in private and public arenas. The streets of the village are teeming with women who obviously are following a rather tight time-schedule. Women of the fishermen's strata in Nazaré do not seem to have time for leisurely strolls, but give the impression of always being in the midst of some important undertaking. This decidedly un-Mediterranean behavior of women contrasts with the more leisurely pace of the men.

Observations at a closer range confirm the superficial impression of the role of women in the affairs of the village. The women are in a true sense the heads of their households, and are not merely responsible for the traditional chores of women—preparation of food, cleaning, and care of children. They represent the household in both public and private matters and are frequently running a business as well. Thus normally they have little time to spare. Socializing with other women is an important part of a woman's role. It requires either that she receives visitors, or herself visits with friends, who are usually close relatives: daughters, sisters, or mother.

The house of the average family rarely consists of more than one room in addition to the kitchen. Most women take pride in keeping their homes clean and tidy, and provided with the latest modern accessories, such as TV, refrigerator, radio, and hi-fi set, in addition to objects of decoration, bric-a-brac, neat bed-covers, and rugs. In order to get these things, a woman is not only prepared to work long hours to earn money, but she is also prepared to incur the risk of a high burden of debt, mostly to relatives and friends. The house is the domain of the women, and outside the bed and the dinner table, the husband does not really fit into the average household. As soon as he gets up in the morning, the husband is expected to leave the house after a lonely and usually rather perfunctory breakfast, consisting of a cup of coffee and a roll. More often than not he will go to his favorite *taberna* where he usually has his first drink. Unless he is busy with his own fishing gear or that of his patron, he will divide his time between his *taberna* and leisurely strolls along the beach.

In order to get a systematic impression of matrimonial life, we shall follow the development of the Nazaré household from the time of its establishment.

HOUSEHOLD ESTABLISHMENT

The Nazarenos marry at a comparatively early age—19 for women and 22 for men. The legal age is 16, a fact very much resented by the women. Not infrequently girls as young as 14 get pregnant, but have to postpone the formal act of marriage until almost a year after the birth of their child. (Consult the tables below.)

This, however, is not regarded as scandalous by the villagers. It is more or less the rule that the girl is pregnant before marriage. I first became aware of this when a woman explained almost proudly that she had not been married as a white bride because she was several months pregnant at the time of the marriage ceremony.

This attitude is also decidedly un-Mediterranean. With my previous experience from fieldwork in Southern Italy (Brøgger 1971), I found her declaration was not merely surprising, but indeed shocking. Among Italian peasants the virginity of

TABLE 2–1

Age	Marriage Men	Women	Union Men	Women
13	–	–	–	1.0
14	–	2.0	1.0	5.0
15	1.0	5.0	2.0	7.0
16	2.0	13.0	3.0	14.0
17	7.0	19.0	9.0	16.0
18	13.0	29.0	11.0	26.0
19	14.0	19.0	16.0	22.0
20	19.0	23.0	15.0	24.0
21	21.0	21.0	23.0	20.0
23	18.0	9.0	17.0	10.0
24	12.0	7.0	12.0	6.0
25	14.0	5.0	13.0	4.0
26	3.0	3.0	4.0	3.0
27	9.0	–	10.0	–
28	5.0	1.0	3.0	1.0
29	3.0	3.0	4.0	3.0
30	4.0	1.0	3.0	2.0
31	1.0	–	1.0	–
32	2.0	1.0	2.0	–
33	1.0	–	1.0	–
35	1.0	1.0	–	–
45	1.0	1.0	–	–
51	1.0	–	–	–
Total	179.0	179.0	179.0	179.0
Average	22.7	20.3	22.3	19.6

This table was based on a sample of 179 couples of the fishing community of Nazaré, in November 1986. The legal age of 16 was established for marriage according to the Código Civil of April 1, 1976. The early marriages according to the table were contracted before 1976.

TABLE 2–2

Age of mother at first child's birth	Frequency
14	1.0
15	2.0
16	6.0
17	8.0
18	21.0
19	28.0
20	21.0
21	20.0
22	13.0
23	16.0
24	8.0
25	9.0
26	8.0
27	1.0
28	0.0
29	1.0
30	5.0
35	1.0
36	1.0
37	1.0
39	1.0
Average	21.4

This table was based on the sample referred to in table 2–1.

their daughters before marriage is a matter of the gravest concern. A boy caught in the act of deflowering a girl without being married in Southern Italy would be in grave danger and run the risk of being shot by a brother or the father if he did not marry the girl. Because the Portuguese, not only through their language but also with regard to customs and beliefs, are close to the Italian peasants, this deviation from the Mediterranean code of honor is striking. The deviation, however, is not as dramatic as one at first is led to believe.

The reason behind the apparent shamelessness is a particular elaboration of the Mediterranean institution of elopement. Elopement in Southern Italy is a most serious matter through which young people challenge the authority of their parents with regard to choice of marriage partner. In Nazaré the elopement has become an unofficial marriage ritual, which from the point of view of the community is regarded as legitimate and as binding as the official act. More than half of the marriages in Nazaré are established through elopement. Of a sample of 56 marriages, 34 started with elopement.

When two young people are showing interest in each other and meeting regularly, they are recognized as *namoradas*. Although these relationships are established without any ritual or formal procedures, the relationship is equal to an engagement. As *namoradas* they will meet in the houses of their respective parents. These chaperoned encounters are supposed to be the only contact between the young couple before the marriage. But it is common knowledge that couples do meet clandestinely. In arranging these extracurricular encounters, they will receive generous help from their friends. They will usually meet in a house where both parents are temporarily out during the day. Granted the active life of the women and the style of life of fishermen, there are plenty of opportunities.

Even if the parents rarely arrange marriages for their children, they commonly take an active interest in their children's choice of partners. It is regarded as the responsibility of the mothers to exert their influence in these matters. This is also a deviation from the Mediterranean custom, where male honor is particularly expressed in the control of the sexual behavior of the women of their household. In Nazaré, however, the fathers will feign ignorance of these matters while their wives are busy scheming. Mothers rarely translate their concern into straightforward well-meaning advice, as is the rule in North European middle class. Rather they will exert their influence in a more oblique way. If they do not approve of the relationship, they will criticize the person in question, emphasize his or her shortcomings, character deficiencies, way of dressing, and the reputation of the partner and his or her family. They will also resort to evil gossip, and there is hardly a person in Nazaré who has never been the subject of this form of character assassination. If the mothers fail to sway their children by these means, they will resort to bad treatment of their children: refuse to talk to them, fail to give them food, and sometimes even beat them. As a last resort they may throw their children out of the house. This, however, is high risk procedure because it may drive the children into the arms of their in-laws. There is ample evidence to suggest that mothers frequently succeed in destroying the relationships they regard as undesirable. They may also have some success in promoting relationships they approve of. In these cases they may secretly promote an elopement.

One case of elopement I had the chance to observe at close range: Mário, 18, established a relationship with Ana, 15, the girl next door. Everyday Ana would come to Mário's house. She did this for some time without the knowledge of her parents, but they eventually discovered what was going on. Since they did not particularly approve of the relationship, Ana's mother tried to get the relationship terminated. She claimed that Ana was too young, barely 15. The main reason, however, was that Mário was not considered a suitable husband for her daughter. He was suffering from a weak spine and was not regarded as particularly intelligent. His family did not have a favorable reputation. His father was an alcoholic but managed to earn a living, and his mother was disliked because she frequently had to borrow money and for this reason presented herself as more miserable than she really was. Both Mário's father and mother were of families with poor reputations. His father was suffering from the low reputation earned by a grandfather who served as the town sweeper, and whose descendants were all known by the nickname *Varedor,* broom. The mother's family was stigmatized because of a somewhat eccentric mother and a notorious alcoholic father who frequently made a fool of himself in public.

Ana's family on the other hand was more reputable and comparatively wealthy because her father was a sailor, and her mother had prepared an impressive trousseau for her. Moreover, she was their only daughter, who with only one brother would share an inheritance of one house and one apartment. It was not beyond her possibilities to get one of the more promising young men from a reputable family. But Ana was determined that she wanted to marry Mário. In order to arrange an elopement, they confided in Mário's younger brother, Joaquim, who was 16 years old. Joaquim kept me informed of the proceedings, at the same time demonstrating how difficult it is to maintain secrets in the village. Joaquim arranged for a taxi to appear in front of the high school, which usually was deserted in the evening. On the chosen day, Joaquim and Mário left the house in the evening "to play foot-ball," and their mother advised them not to be late. I had the distinct impression that the mother was perfectly aware of what was going on, and that her admonitions were merely make-believe. The taxi-driver took Mário and Ana to the village São Pedro Moel about 10 kilometers to the north, where they rented a room in a reasonable *pensão*. Joaquim followed the couple in order to know their whereabouts because he was going to serve as a messenger, keeping the couple informed of the reactions of her family.

Ana's parents became very upset because of the elopement. The mother declared that her daughter had forfeited her trousseau, and her father said that he would never again see the daughter in his house. When the couple returned to Nazaré after a couple of days, they were accommodated by a cousin of Ana's mother, and in the evening they opened the negotiations. Ana came to Mário's house at ten o'clock at night and asked his mother to plead their case. She refused, but advised her to ask her mother's cousin to talk to her parents. The mother's cousin accepted the assignment, went to see Ana's mother, and asked her insistently to receive her daughter. The mother was easy to persuade, but her father would not give in so easily. A cousin of Ana had to be summoned; she pleaded with the father and maintained that he would solve no problems if he refused to accept them. "They are not the only ones who have escaped," she argued. "Many young people of their age are eloping, and after all, she is your daughter."

After a protracted argument, the father gave in, and Ana and Mário were received in the house late at night. The next day during breakfast, Mário approached his prospective father-in-law, and they had a friendly talk. In the eyes of the villagers, Mário and Ana were now properly married, living together in her mother's house as husband and wife. Later Ana's mother rented an apartment for them, and after a few months it became known that Ana was pregnant. This did not cause anyone to raise an eyebrow in spite of the fact that they in the official sense were not legally married. In case of elopement, it is not customary to arrange a formal wedding-party. It is often maintained that many parents secretly induce the young folks to elope in order to save the expenses. This may be true in many cases. However, the reasons why the elopement has become a recognized marriage form among the fishermen are more complex.

In Turkey, elopement is, according to Grønnhaug (1969), arranged more or less like a theatrical performance. The girl is actually abducted by the prospective groom and his friends. In the majority of cases it is more make-believe. It is, in other words, a ritual, a ritual that clearly relates to the management of human emotions. In a patriarchal society like that of the Turks, where the male lineage is the

A proper marriage in church, um casamento bonito, *presumably not the result of an elopement. The bride is 16, the bridegroom 19.*

backbone of the community, marriage implies the transfer of rights from one male lineage to another. This transfer, of course, is not like any other business deal. Both human affection and male pride are involved. It is painful to give up a daughter and a sister to another male and his lineage. The elopement serves to conceal the painful consent of the bride's male guardians. In a way it expresses that they in fact had no real choice in giving up their control. In a make-believe way it indicates that permission was not given voluntarily, and as such it is a tribute both to their affections for the bride and to her feelings. She is, as it were, not given up without a fight, and a mock battle is in fact often part of the ritual of elopement.

In Southern Italy, as in France (Wylie 1964), elopement implies a genuine challenge to the authority of the parents. Indeed, the institution of elopement in patrilineal societies testifies to a persistent conflict between love and strategy. The recognition of the elopement is a tribute by strategy to love in societies where the parents are in supreme control of their children and their matrimonial arrangements. Elopement provides an example in the support of Ruth Benedict's classical analysis of patterns of culture (1935). In the Mediterranean area from Turkey to Portugal, elopement is found as a cultural institution, with different emphasis and elaboration. It may be regarded as a tribute to the position of the family, particularly to the male authority. It provides an ultimate possibility for a compromise between love and strategy. In Portugal it has become the recognized form of marriage at the folk level. This indicates that love holds more importance than strategy in the Portuguese case.

The negotiations upon the return of the eloped couple also have a make-believe quality. If male authority had been seriously challenged in the case of Ana and Mário, the father would probably have been a little more persistent in his opposition than was the case. In actual fact, the father has practically no authority at all. The tribute to his authority thus may be regarded as a tribute to a Mediterranean ideology of male superiority. The position of authority is actually in the hands of the women, and the source of this power is the predominantly female control of housing. However, parental control in a community of fishermen hardly reaches the strength it has in an agricultural community, where access to land is at stake. The fact that access to the sea is not in the hands of the fathers is probably one of the reasons for their peripheral position in the Nazareno households.

The local elaboration of an element of a Mediterranean marriage custom that traditionally was marginal in peasant communities is consonant with the facts of conjugal life in Nazaré. Through the elopement, some homage is paid to the rights of the families to have an influence in the establishment of a new household, and at the same time the independent choice of the young is recognized. In general terms, elopement in Nazaré may thus be regarded as a sensible compromise between the individualism of modern times and the communal nature of the traditional marriage, which is still recognized in Nazaré. Although the elopement symbolically indicates that the girl's family transfers its rights in her to the husband and his family, this proves to be a superficial tribute to an ideology which in other ways is unimportant. In actual fact, it is in most cases the family of the bridegroom that is giving up its rights.

Behind the somewhat urban surface of life in Nazaré, an almost tribal organization can be recognized with regard to family and marriage-arrangements. As we shall see, tendencies towards the formation of matrilineages exist among the strata of fishermen in Nazaré. Marriages, therefore, are less individualistic than in modern, industrial societies. Some of the old ground rules of lineage societies seem to exert themselves in the Nazareno context.

MATRILOCAL RESIDENCE AND EXTENDED FAMILIES

A marriage relationship between two families in Nazaré does not establish any measure of cooperation and visiting. On the contrary, the respective in-laws of the newly established couple seemingly take great care to avoid each other. In pre-modern agricultural societies the in-laws commonly lived in different communities, and therefore did not face the problem of bumping into each other in the course of everyday life. If they interacted at all, it would have been at the level of politeness and ritual. In Nazaré, of course, the wife-givers, or rather husband-givers, and receiving families do not reside in different communities. As a response to the potential conflicts between in-laws an informal system of avoidance is maintained. In accordance with the female dominance in Nazaré, a tendency toward matrilocal residence can be recognized. If at all possible, a newly wed couple will be accommodated by the mother of the girl. Since the real-estate market in Nazaré is a capitalist enterprise, the living arrangements of the families cannot be expected to demonstrate the actual preference among the average families. Only families of means can make arrangements according to their wishes, and these cases confirm the preference for matrilocal residence in marriage. Although living conditions rarely admit extended families, a clear tendency in the same direction can be observed as well for families who are dependent upon rented facilities.

In a sample of 26 families, the tendency to seek out location close to the wife's mother is clearly demonstrated:

	Those with	Percentage of those with
Daughters married	20	
Daughters close	11	55
Sons married	19	
Sons close	5	26
Wife's sisters	24	
Wife's sisters close	18	75
Wife's brothers	35	
Wife's brothers close	7	20
Husband's sisters	27	
Husband's sisters close	13	48
Husband's brothers	26	
Husband's brothers close	8	30
Wife's parents	26	
Wife's parents close	14	50
Husband's parents	26	
Husband's parents close	5	19

As can be seen from the table, 55 percent of the daughters were living close to their mothers compared to 26 percent in the case of the sons. In the case of the wife's sisters, the situation is even more pronounced, with a percentage of 75 compared to 20 for wife's brothers. Obviously, the choice of residence results in a concentration of close, female relatives around the maternal household.

Relationships between the cousins also confirm the matrilocal tendency. A group of 16 boys asked about their first cousins revealed a comparative lack of knowledge about the cousins on their father's side. They reported to know 12 cousins from the uterine side and only 4 from their father's side. Of course, this is not a proof of a higher frequency of interaction between uterine kins, but it is at least a result of the proximity of living quarters.

Among the better-off fish-sellers, or *peixeiras*, several cases of joint property between sisters were found. In these cases matrilineally extended families were established and a structure similar to a lineage emerged. The case of Maria Cândida may serve as a clearcut example. With her sister Maria Antonia, she bought a small seven unit apartment house where she owns four of the apartments. Maria Cândida lives in one of the apartments with her husband and her youngest son. Her oldest son is, as is to be expected, living with his wife close to his mother-in-law. Her two daughters are living in two of the other apartments with their husbands and children. The last of her four apartments is let during the summer, when her eldest daughter is expected to move out to a provisory cabin, a *cabana*, so that her apartment, which is the biggest, can be rented to tourists in the season from June through August. The present state of this matrilineally extended family is shown in the following sketch:

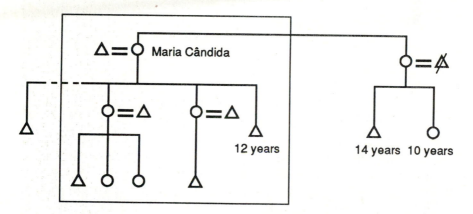

A clear matrilineal pattern has been established, and Maria Cândida is the undisputed ruler of her husband and her married daughters. She also dominates her younger sister. Although each married couple has its own kitchen and purse, her psychological presence makes the term *extended family* justified.

Maria Cândida gives regular gifts of fish to her daughters and also some financial assistance. In turn she expects a fair measure of submission. Sometimes she will eat with one of her daughters, and her son of 12 will frequently have dinner with one of his married sisters. Maria Cândida's husband is a fisherman who works with a small crew of other fishermen. He does not have his own boat or nets, but will get his part of the catch, according to custom. He is completely dominated by his wife, and from time to time she scolds him. On these occasions he will rarely raise his voice, and only when drunk will he demonstrate a measure of self-assertion.

Maria Cândida's moods are a general topic of concern in the compound, and her daughters sometimes voice resentment about her dominance. But being dependent upon her, they will not question her authority. Her sons-in-law also act respectfully in her presence, and are gradually being incorporated into the matrifocal lineage segment.

When Maria Cândida enters the compound, she always emphasizes her presence with a lot of movement and talking. One typical day, she shouted to her youngest daughter from the window of her apartment:

"Did you serve lunch to your father?"
"No, he was in a very bad mood."

Addressing her eldest daughter in the apartment below:

"Why haven't you prepared the fish?"

Talking loudly to herself:

"It is all on my cost." *(É tudo à custa da mesma.)*

To her youngest son:

"Lionel, come and have your dinner."

Lionel, from his sister's apartment:

"I am having dinner."

To Lionel:

"That is good for you." (Her meaning being that everybody is taken care of except her and her husband.)

After having asserted her authority in this manner, she starts to talk in a more pleasant way with her eldest daughter. She is able to terrorize the whole compound from the window of her apartment. When she starts to sing *fados,* the nostalgic Portuguese folk songs, everybody knows that tension is building up and an eruption may be forthcoming.

The style of female authority in Nazaré does not emphasize dignity and calm. It is frequently expressed in a nagging way and with an ample display of emotions. This is in tune with the dominant style of interaction in the village. This style is above all personal and engaged, and emotions are always close to the surface in most everyday encounters. Strength of personality often seems more important than strength of argument. This style of interaction clearly reflects the lack of recognized formal leadership in the community of fishermen. Social dominance therefore is not so much based on general principles as on charismatic display. Speaking in the terms of role theory, interaction calls for an involvement of the whole person, and is scarcely restricted to one particular aspect of a repertory of roles. We shall return to this question later, but in the present context it is sufficient to emphasize that female authority is unusually strong and usually sufficiently to dominate the men. It is not uncommon for a woman to ask her husband to shut up, which he normally will do if he is not drunk or in an unusually aggressive frame of mind.

Although women usually also dominate their sons, they do not like the idea of having other women in command of them. When sons marry, they are frequently warned against submission. *"Nunca deixes ninguém pôr-te o pé em cima do queixaço"* ("Don't ever let anyone put their feet on your neck") is a common warning to young men in the process of getting married. This warning, however, is usually given in vain. As soon as the new household is established, the bride, usually spurred by her mother and her aunts, struggles to get the upper hand. Since

The Nazareno women often dominate their men. The demeanor of this formid-
able widow is expressive of their strength and self-assurance.

the husband in the majority of cases will be surrounded by his wife's family, he is in
a somewhat exposed position. This is particularly the case if he becomes part of the
matrilineally extended family.

The women rule the back streets of Nazaré, which serve as an extension of their households.

THE DOMESTICATION OF HUSBANDS

Although the art of dominating males may not have been consciously elaborated, a somewhat standard procedure can be observed. The first year of marriage normally tends to be quite turbulent. Young men will frequently complain of their wives' unpredictable moody spells. For no obvious reason a wife may meet her husband with a gloomy face when he comes home, and give him the feeling of having committed some particularly disgusting offense. Nazareno men seem to be quite vulnerable to this type of emotional strategy, which instantly puts them on the defensive. This may in fact be true of men in general, but perhaps the majority of fishermen in Nazaré are particularly vulnerable because their income is unpredictable, often meager, which makes them dependent upon the resources of their wives.

During the first year of marriage the emotional brain-washing of the husbands is usually combined with assaults on their families. Wives and mothers-in-law tend to resent it that their husbands have frequent contacts with their own families. Because the husband's relationship to his mother may give him an independent source of emotional strength, contact between mother and son is particularly resented. In cases where the husband becomes part of the matrilineally extended family, all the women will join forces in giving his mother the cold shoulder if she visits her son. It takes great personal strength to endure the chilly reception she will receive if she ever appears, and few mothers are able to stand up against this. The same holds for the father, but he will rarely if ever visit his married sons. It is not uncommon for a father to not even know the exact address of his married son. A wife normally resents her husband's visits to his old home, and she may punish him with a particularly violent tantrum. In most cases the wives will succeed in alienating the husband from his family of origin, and he will become more or less incorporated in the family of his wife.

Mothers frequently express great bitterness about the psychological loss of their sons. This, however, does not prevent them from playing the same game with their own sons-in-law. In this effort they will enlist the collaboration of their daughters, and they will also resort to gossip to damage daughters-in-law and their mothers.

Nazarenos will normally have a file of dark information on most of their family, friends, and acquaintances. There will often be a kernel of truth in the gossip, but there is also a considerable amount of genuine disinformation in circulation. The dark information is normally circulating in a clandestine way as classified information. But in the event of open quarrels, which frequently occur in public, women will instantly declassify even the most damaging news and throw it in the face of their opponents. A frequent saying is:

Ralham as comadres,
sabem-se as verdades.

When the godmothers quarrel,
  you will know the truth.

This manipulation explains the ritual avoidance maintained between the respective families of a married couple. At the baptism of the first child, the husband's parents normally will not show up. With good reason they are much less concerned with the children of their sons than of their daughters. Possibly to soothe the pain at this alienation, they will quote a common proverb:

Filhos das minhas filhas, meus netos são,
filhos dos meus filhos—serão ou não.

Children of my daughters are truly my grandchildren,
  the children of my sons are possibly my grandchildren or possibly not.

A fact that makes the psychological loss of sons painful is that female control is not in acccordance with the official ideology. The Nazarenos subscribe to the common Mediterranean ideas of male dominance. During marriage negotiations lip-service is paid to this ideology, and when asked, both men and women will claim that the men are in control. An unusually large discrepancy is thus maintained between ideals and reality. This tension is undoubtedly one of the reasons why social life in Nazaré has a high-strung quality that makes emotional eruptions almost the order of the day. The Nazarenos are aware of this and will explain that the village is full of nerves. Because the tensions created by their family system are not covered by any rules or recognized forms of ritual avoidance, each person has to work out a personal solution. It becomes a matter of personal management of emotions and not a fulfillment of culturally defined procedures.

A conscious ideology in tune with the facts of female dominance merely exists in a rudimentary way. But a rather significant interpretation of the process of procreation emerged during a discussion about inheritance. The object of discussion was a gold chain in the possession of Ana.

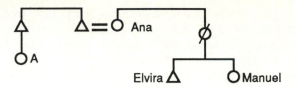

The family of her husband and their children, A, claimed their share in the gold chain. Manuel, however, denied their rights and maintained that he and Elvira were her true relatives:

A criança desenvolve-se dentro da mãe. Onde vai buscar o sangue é a carne de que é feita? É à propria mãe.

Because a child develops in the body of a woman, from where will it get blood and meat if not from the mother?

This recalls the ideas of the matrilineal Trobrianders (Malinowski 1929) who claimed ignorance of the father's role in conception. It contrasts also dramatically from the idea common elsewhere in the Mediterranean that the child grows from the seed planted by the father in the womb of the mother.

THE POSITION OF FATHERS IN A COMPARATIVE PERSPECTIVE

The dominant position of women appears to be a firmly entrenched culture trait in Nazaré. Behind the surface of a superficial, Mediterranean ideology, an equivocal reality of *matrifocality* (Tanner 1974) exists together with an almost fully fledged matrilineal family organization. The term *matrifocality* was chosen by anthropologists as an alternative to *matriarchy* in order to describe female dominance. The knowledge of women's role in social life increased rapidly as a large number of female scholars entered the rank of anthropologists from the beginning of the 1970s. Because the information gathered by social anthropologists is strongly dependent upon the social role they are able to play as resident strangers, the male knowledge of the women's world of course was rather restricted. Because anthropology with a few prominent exceptions had been dominated by men, the role of women in what we may refer to as ethnographic-societies was sometimes overlooked and often not recognized. However, even in periods of extreme male dominance, an idea of a matriarchal society persisted in the Western mind, possibly as a legacy of the Greek myth of the Amazons. Whatever the source of the idea, it promoted reflections on the possible existence of female dominated societies in a distant, historical past or in some not yet discovered corner of the world. The idea was explored by Bachoven in his classical work "Das Mutterrecht" and seriously considered by Engels in his book on the origin of marriage (1881). The term *matriarchy*, therefore, already had a history when the nature of female power in societies was explored by professional female anthropologists. Because female dominance is not expressed as a mirror image of patriarchy, the term *matrifocality* was coined.

In a matrifocal society the ritual status of women is equal to that of men. This also implies that a woman's role as mother is publicly recognized in a different manner than in modern bourgeois society as it existed up until the middle of the twentieth century. Because of the privatization of the nuclear family, the role of the women was exercised in the privacy of the homes. In spite of both poetic and sentimental recognition of motherhood, its relevance somehow was restricted to the private scene of the household. With the disruption of the communal living of the middle ages, the doors of bourgeois homes were closed to society at large and the female often lost touch with the public world of power, influence, and economy. Although a woman could be extremely powerful within the confines of the nuclear family, her importance as social being and as mother did not reach beyond the sphere of the household. The idea of her influence was sometimes described as *mommism,* and as such was stultified and not accepted as legitimate within the public sphere.

Matrifocal societies have been discovered in many different cultures in Asia, Africa, and the contemporary United States. For example, in Indonesia the Minangkabau, through the studies of H. Geertz, were recognized as a society in which the women participated as the equals of men both economically and politically. Even in strictly patriarchal societies in West-Africa, like the Yoruba, powerful women dominated both their households and the markets. Although men were the official masters of polygynous households, the women were in charge of their own realms not restricted by the walls of the compounds. As operators on the rural

Women do not participate in the fishing at sea, but the fishing from the shore is partly dominated by the women. No one will doubt the authority of this woman.

markets, they gained economic independence to a degree that made it possible for them to compete with the men. With their economic power they were even able to sustain the somewhat curious institution of female marriages. An economically successful woman was sometimes able both to fulfill her duty as a legitimate wife of her husband and to contract a marriage with a younger woman. This was not a sexual union, however, and should not be confused with lesbian relationships. The purpose of the union was to beget children. The control of these children was the sole responsibility of the woman. Through these children they were able to control marriages in the same way as their husbands.

The matrifocal nature of the society of fishermen is not only realized in the female dominance of the economy, but also through the legitimacy of the role of mothers outside the sphere of the household. In modern Western society, it is common for boys to refer to the authority of their fathers in discussion with their peers (I have to ask my father). In Nazaré it is more likely that a boy will refer to the authority of his mother (I have to ask my mother). Boys are expected to be under the authority of their mothers, and no one is accused of being a sissy or a mama's boy if they recognize this in public.

COMMUNAL NATURE OF VILLAGE LIFE

Not only the female dominance makes Nazaré a special case on the European scene. Equally conspicuous in the eyes of a modern, middle-class observer is the com-

The authority of the women is not restricted to the household. Nazareno boys will usually refer to the authority of their mothers rather than their fathers. The female presence in public is typical of Nazaré.

munal nature of village life and the lack of privatization of the family. Social historians like Stone (1977) and Shorter (1975) have demonstrated how the European nuclear family at the dawn of our modern era closed the door to the community at large and established a secluded private sphere outside the ears and eyes of the community. Stone has pointed out how this seclusion in a manner of speaking increased the emotional temperature in the household. Partly isolated from kith and kin, the spouses had more time for each other and for their children. Of particular importance was the transformation of the marriage into an exclusive dyadic relationship of great emotional significance. Before the privatization of the nuclear family, the spouses were normally more involved with their respective gender-cultures than with each other. They were operating in two different worlds and had few opportunities to be alone with each other and develop a mutual relationship of confidence.

The social repercussions of The Great Transformation mentioned in the introduction changed all that. As money and markets deprived neighborhoods of their economic significance, the communal life of the village lost its strength. People became less dependent upon each other, but also more lonely, or, in the jargon of modern sociology, they became "alienated" from each other. This was compensated for by the establishment of the *companionate marriage,* where a close friendship between husband and wife prevails at the cost of the relationship to their respective gender-cultures (see also page 52). Social networks became less comprehensive, but what was lost in numbers was gained in intensity, with the marriage partnership becoming the most important relationship of all. In the communal period of village life in Europe the energy of social relationships was spread thin over a number of partners. But with the gradual disintegration of the close folk community of *l'ancien régime,* life became less dependent upon a collective of fellow citizens and was concentrated on a limited number of close, dyadic relationships with spouse, children and friends. Nazaré, however, as far as marriage and social relationships are concerned, remains a folk community, in spite of the fact that the forces of modernization are obvious on the village scene. Economically Nazaré is not operating like a folk community. Most of the important things in life—house, equipment and to a large degree food—have to be negotiated through the market. Although a case can be made that the fishermen are not salaried workers, the presence in Nazaré of comparatively large-scale fishing enterprises established by capitalist entrepreneurs justifies the claim that the fishing is industrialized in the structural sense of the word. Although the entrepreneurs themselves are active leaders of their enterprises, and the fishermen receive a part of the catch rather than a fixed salary, a large percentage of the fishermen do not participate in family enterprises.

In spite of all the features of modernization in Nazaré, the companionate marriage so important in the formation of the modern, Western mind has not developed. Neither has the nuclear family been privatized in the same degree as is common in the industrialized world. The private scene is of little importance compared to the communal life of the Nazarenos, who refer to the collective as the *praia*. The *praia* literally means "the beach," and this choice of term emphasizes the beach as the main focus of social life.

MATRIFOCALITY AND THE POSITION OF HUSBANDS

Comparative evidence suggests that it is the female dominance in Nazaré that has prevented the privatization of the nuclear family and the consequent development of the companionate marriage. It is a general observation that the role of husbands in matrifocal societies tends to be marginal inside the household, which is definitely the case in Nazaré. Among the Minangkabau, for example, the main role of the husband is to provide cash through migrant labor. When he returns to his home with hard-earned cash, he is received as an honored guest. As most house-guests know, however, prolonged visits are rarely appreciated. When the money is spent, he is expected to leave the household in order to provide more cash. The peripheral role of the men in the black ghettoes in the United States also seems to be related to low earning-power of the males and to the strong position of women. Girls growing up in the ghetto are trained to fend for themselves. Although the situation in the ghetto, accordingly to a commonly held opinion in the present day United States, is primarily due to sexism and male irresponsibility, comparative information suggests that the first explanation is closer to the truth.

The famous case of the Nayars of the Malbar coast of India (Schneider and Gough 1961) throws interesting light on the marriage institution as such. Among traditional Nayars before modernization, the husbands had no role to play within the household at all. In fact, there were no husbands in the conventional sense of the word. It is true that girls were symbolically married off to high-caste men, but the marriage was never consummated and the "husband" had no role to play within the household at all. He did not father the children. This task was left to lovers which served as *genitors,* but never as *paters*. The male role was played by the brothers, who in the role of mothers' brothers were the executives of their sisters' properties. The traditional Nayars could probably not be described as matrifocal, yet their system demonstrated some of the basic facts of human family life and procreation. The simple fact that the women bear children gives them a different position than the males with regard to offspring. In order to get access to their own children, men have to establish a workable relationship with their children's mothers. The woman, on the other hand, does not need the permanent presence of a man in her life in order to have children. All that is needed is sperm, which is a more readily available material than the ovum. As the Nayars have demonstrated, women do not need a husband in the social sense at all. Marriage, then, may in a certain sense be regarded as a male institution. It seems to be the rule that matrilinear societies are reluctant to accept men from outside as full-fledged members of the family and tribe. Among the matrilinear, Dobuans (Fortune 1963) in the Pacific as well as among the Yao of Southern Africa (Mitchell 1956), in-marrying males are referred to by a term that may be adequately translated as "billy goats." In a patrilinear system, on the other hand, the breeding of children requires the permanent presence of women from a different clan. Although patrilineal societies may exploit the women in many ways, they must for their very existence accept them as full-fledged members of the tribe.

The basic facts of procreation make the position of fathers quite vulnerable vis-a-vis their children. Their position requires a particular type of social organization in order to be sustained. The father's position is strongest in cases where the male lineage monopolizes the productive resources, as among tribal agriculturalists.

Where the productive resources are monopolized by the female lineage, the type of local organization to a certain degree determines the position of fathers. Among the Trobrianders, for instance, the position of fathers seems to be emotionally satisfactory, but the authority is in the hands of the mother's brother. Among the Dobuans it is precarious when the husband lives in his wife's village, just as among the Cewa. He is certainly marginal among the Ashanti and was completely absent among the Nayars. In cases of matrilineal descent and inheritance the father has strong competition from the mother's brother. This of course reminds us of the fact that matrilineal inheritance does not automatically imply matrifocality. In many matrilineal societies power is firmly in the hands of the males.

We do not yet know how and under which conditions matrifocality emerges. But the majority of cases suggests that if the women are in control of essential resources, such as agricultural production and houses among the Minangkabau, and at the same time male presence in the local community is somewhat lower than the female presence, matrifocality may emerge. Matrifocality seems to be dependent upon the reduced presence of the mother's brother. In Minangkabau, he is either married into a clan different from his own or absent as a migrant laborer. In the black ghetto there are hardly any resources which are in the control of the males, which leaves both the husband, or genitor, and the mother's brother without possibilities.

It seems to be generally true that the father's position in a matrifocal household is marginal. Among the Minangkabau as well as among the Nazarenos and in the black ghetto, fathers are under the dominion of women within the framework of the household. In Nazaré they are simply not tolerated at home during the daytime unless they are in bed sleeping. Husbands will congregate in the *tabernas* and on the *praia* and only come home for their meals.

It seems fairly obvious that privatization of the nuclear family under these circumstances would have little meaning. Privatization of the nuclear family certainly requires a secure position both for husband and wife. The precarious position of fathers in matrifocal societies is today repeated in modern Western society with the liberation of women. With the growing independence of women, the patriarchal traditions of the Euro-American family are efficiently challenged. Characteristically, the precarious position of the men in the household emerges, resulting in a large number of families in which the children grow up without the presence of fathers. Somewhat exaggeratedly, it may be suggested that in the transformation of the modern family currently in process, the man may in certain cases be reduced to the role of the impregnator, as among the Nayars.

In Nazaré the husband has undeniable right of presence in the household, but without the patriarchal privileges of the traditional Mediterranean family. Compared to husbands in full-fledged matrilinear systems, such as the Dobuans or the Yao, for example, they reach a comparatively high level of acceptance. This is obviously because the male members of the matrilineage leave the compound and its management to the women at marriage. In this respect the Nazarenos are more matriarchal than either of the societies in the tribal examples; because of the actual female power, the in-marrying males do not represent a real challenge to their brothers-in-law.

Because there are no resources comparable to tribal estates, lineages exceeding three generations do not emerge in Nazaré. Also, because inheritance is bilateral, the situation in Nazaré cannot be described as unequivocally matrilinear. The system may, however, be described as a latent matrilineal system. Because it is part of the bureaucratic state and constrained both by the national laws and a capitalist system, the small matrifocal groups, or extended families, are not allowed to grow and develop their latent matrilinear tendencies through the generations. The full-fledged matrilineally extended families, apart from being comparatively rare in Nazaré, dissolve with the death of the dominant mother, when also the sons appear to claim their share in the inheritance. This happens in spite of the fact that sons usually become more or less alienated from their families of origin.

After the turbulent first year of marriage, the husband is usually broken in and resigns himself to the dominance of his wife and his mother-in-law. But this is not a rule without exceptions. The exceptions, however, also present a distinct pattern. The most successful of the fishermen sometimes manage to establish themselves as masters of their households, thus realizing normally subdued Mediterranean values. Ownership of larger vessels, which represent a considerable investment, is the male answer to the *peixeiras,* the fish-sellers. These men become truly rich, even according to national standards, and can emerge as a clearly visible elite among the fishermen. It is no coincidence that the majority of *mestres,* as they are referred to, more often than not have powerful personalities and are easily recognized by their self-assured demeanor among the majority of meeker colleagues. Probably because of the charismatic basis of their enterprises, wealthy dynasties of masters have failed to develop. The son of a rich and successful *mestre* will often become an ordinary fisherman himself, unless through a superior education and network he is shunted off to the bourgeoisie. This has prevented the emergence of in-stitutionalized strata among the fishermen and accounts for the maintenance of the egalitarian nature of the fisherman's culture.

What our brief comparative excursion clearly demonstrates is that the privatized nuclear family that has been the rule in Euro-America for many generations has been based on patriarchal values. When it emerged in the wake of industrialization a certain degree of male dominance was already entrenched. With the increasing role of monetarization, men in many cases sustained a virtual monopoly on the monetary income of the family. Given the full responsibility for the maintenance of the family, and being the representative of the extra-familiar relationships of his household, the man sought to continue the patrilineal tradition rooted in the history of the family institution in Europe (Stone, 1977). This dominance is probably not due solely to the dominant nature of men as such; it probably emerged from a need to control the childbearing women so that the lineage might be reproduced. This is part and parcel of the problem exogamous patrilinear communities face with regard to reproduction. Unlike matrilineally organized communities, which in theory need no more than male sperm, a fact of which the Nayar took full advantage, they struggle to fully incorporate the in-marrying partner, i.e., the woman.

These facts should correct some common misconceptions on male dominance fostered by Engels (1881) in his influential work on the origin of the human family. Engels maintained that monogamy and male dominance was established because men wished to assure themselves of the authenticity of their offspring in biological terms. Engels was right with regard to the need to control the women in patriarchal societies, but he was wrong with regard to its cause. Men were probably not concerned with their role as genitors, but with their rights in children, which in fact required physical control of their wives.

During my fieldwork among the patrilineal Sidamo of Ethiopia (Brøgger 1986), I discovered that even strong male authority was not always sufficient to prevent the newly wed women from running away and hiding in the garden of their fathers. I personally negotiated the return of the wife of my assistant, which required a slight increase in the brideprice.

With the dissolution of the medieval corporate community, the men withdrew from their peer groups into the companionate marriage, keeping their traditional authority more or less intact. This authority was in fact a necessary precondition for the companionate nuclear family. Without this authority, the privatization of the family would have been impossible, because only through a comparatively high degree of control were males able to maintain a psychological niche within the family.

Only if men have a crucial role in the economic maintenance of the family, will they be able to keep a dominant position. As the comparative material suggests, a woman will tend to regard a man as a source of disturbance in the daily routine of the household if his contribution to the maintenance is insignificant.

This is not quite the situation in Nazaré, although the earnings of the women in many cases are much higher than that of their husbands. The economic performance of the man is only sufficient to keep his position within the household, and it is a somewhat subdued position. This is the most likely reason why the traditional family has been maintained in Nazaré. Because of the female dominance, men have not been able to withdraw from their peer groups, and the companionate marriage has failed to develop. It should be added that it is traditional only in the sense that the tie between the spouses has failed to take precedence over the tie to the community.

FAMILY LIFE, EMOTIONS, AND INTIMACY

As we shall see in the following, the emotional climate characteristic of the middle class family, with its accumulation of emotional energy on a restricted nucleus of parents and children, does not prevail in Nazaré. That particular emotional climate seems to be dependent upon the companionate marriage, which emerged during the eighteenth century. It is this intimacy that more than anything else has produced what we recognize as the modern mentality. In the psychological greenhouse of the nuclear family, not only has emotional bonding flourished, but with it has come an increasing awareness of humanistic values. The psychological development of children, as well as their education, has become an urgent concern. Nourished by the affective attention of caring parents, the growing personality has reached a higher level of self-awareness and strength of ego. Combined with formal scholastic training and emphasis on manners, moral responsibility and personal hygiene, the emotional investment in the offspring has produced the modern personality.

The absence of the companionate marriage in Nazaré is of particular consequence for the relationship between the spouses and between the father and the
children. This is not to say that couples are not devoted to each other, but that they
spend less time in each other's company and are less concerned with the conscious
expression of romantic love than companionate marriage partners. As Shorter
(1975) has demonstrated convincingly, romantic love became the cornerstone of the
companionate marriage, and several generations of artists and writers have contributed to the elaboration of these complex emotions.

The Nazarenos have also been exposed to the culture of romantic love, which
has definitely contributed to the current form of courtship. Young people are
expected to, and do, fall in love with each other, and the choice of mate is left to the
discretion of the young themselves. In this respect Nazaré is dancing to the modern
tunes. But once marriage has been established, the couple is less concerned with the
explorations of their mutual feelings than in standard modern marriages. Compared
to the modern bourgeois pattern, couples in Nazaré do not develop the exclusive
dyadic qualities that are the hallmark of the companionate marriage. They do not
withdraw into the privacy of their homes at marriage. Neither will they demonstrate
their affection in front of others. Few efforts are expended to establish the idyllic
privacy of the middle class homes.

The house is the habitat of the women, but as has already been made clear, they
are by no means restricted to the house. Although it is one of their important arenas,
the home is not restricted to an intimate circle of friends and relatives, but open
more or less to the whole neighborhood. Characteristically the doors are usually not
locked and often remain wide open as long as there is somebody at home. Great
efforts are spent to keep the house tidy and attractive. The need to keep the house
presentable is one of the reasons given for keeping the male members of the
household away most of the time during daytime. The house, then, is not primarily
the arena of the family, but of the collective of women of the neighborhood.
Although some may be closer friends than others, exclusive, dyadic friendships
hardly seem to exist.

Generally speaking life in the household arena has the same collective quality as
life in the more obviously public arenas of the *tabernas* and the *praia*. The home
may in fact be described as a semipublic arena. But the terms *private* and *public*
somehow seem to be less applicable among the Nazareno fishermen than is normally the case in Western society today. What we normally regard as strictly separate
arenas of social life are less dichotomized in Nazaré. Compared to the situation in
the modern urban society the home seems to be less private and the public arenas
less public. The key to this seemingly paradoxical statement is that a similar code of
behavior applies in both habitats. The interaction in the house is less private and
intimate and the interaction on the public front is less formal than is normally the
case in the urban society. This lack of dichotomy was sometimes clearly demonstrated in the morning when children and women could be seen bringing freshly
baked bread from the shop to their houses merely dressed in their pajamas. In my
eyes this was as if the intimacy of the bedroom and highly private arena was brought
into the cobblestoned street. For a moment it was as if the neighborhood was
transformed into one big family and it gave me a strange feeling of warm togetherness.

This, however, was much of an illusion based on my own culture-bound interpretation of the behavior. It was based on my own experience of secluded family life. To appear outside even the bedroom in pajamas in the middle-class neighborhood of my own childhood was almost inconceivable. To appear in public in pajamas would have been little better than parading in the underwear. Although I should have known better as an anthropologist, the customs of my own neighborhood somehow in that moment appeared to me as the law of nature. I had observed similar behavior in an African village in Sidamo, but with attires so different from the European fashion that it did not make the same impression. It was the fact that the Portuguese were so clearly European in their physical appearance as well as in the fashion of their dress that made the difference in custom so conspicuous. In less emotional terms the observation demonstrated that what to me appeared as intimacy did not have the same meaning to the Portuguese, and I gradually came to the conclusion that the very dimension of intimacy was less developed in the Nazareno neighborhood than I was used to. I made a similar observation on the beach where the fishermen sometimes appeared in their underwear when helping their comrades to push their fishing vessels across the forbidding waves into the open sea. When I later commented on their special underwear, the *cerolas,* one of the fishermen, without the faintest sign of shyness, opened his pants to demonstrate the quality of its material.

Another testimony to the lack of private intimacy of the household was presented one day when our neighbor across the street started to cry out of the window. She was lecturing in a high complaining pitch, which made it difficult for me to grasp her message, and I had to call an interpreter. It appeared that her husband had stolen some of her hidden savings, money she had saved for Christmas, which her husband certainly would squander. She reached out for all the sympathy she could get from the neighbors, and went on for more than an hour, shouting out the amount over and over again. Since this happened during the first months of my fieldwork, I imagined the woman to be crazy. But I soon realized that this display of what in my parts of the world would have remained a dark family secret was not at all uncommon, although it must be admitted that this particular woman was somewhat eccentric.

Metaphorically speaking, this lack of boundary between the public and the household arenas prevents the accumulation of emotional forces that a stricter privacy facilitates. It is as if the emotional energy is dissipated in all directions. The "emotional temperature" in the community at large is certainly higher than on the official arenas of big cities, but at the cost of the emotional energy of the households. The emotional resources of an individual are restricted. If a human being spends most of his emotional energy on his wife and family, he clearly has less to spare for others. Likewise, a husband who is living for his career and spends most of his time away from home and may even have an affair or two with other women has less to give to his wife and children. It is sometimes maintained that it is not the quantity of time spent in a relationship, but its quality that counts. But the time spent in a relationship is at least an indication of its emotional importance.

Judged on the basis of time the husband spends with his family he certainly appears marginal in the household. The same, however, seems to be the case with boys above 12 years of age. Boys are certainly closer to their mothers than they are to their fathers. But mothers certainly have a strong preference for girls, a preference that is rarely compensated for by fathers' preference for boys. Fathers normally remain distant from their children and certainly do not appear to be accomplished child psychologists or pedagogues. It may be unfair to say that they appear to be clumsy with their children, but they do not regard the children as their main responsibility. That is primarily left to the mothers, which seems logical granted the fathers' marginal position in the family. Nazareno men often criticize their fathers for having been too harsh, and tend to favor their mothers, but they have also problems with their mothers, who somehow seem to lose interest in them when they approach puberty. In spite of this, the relationship to their mothers is probably the most intimate relationship they will ever have.

The closest dyadic bond in the family is that between mother and daughter. In the terminology of the Chinese-American anthropologist Francis Hsu this would certainly count as the "dominant kinship-relationship" in Nazaré. The relationship between mother and daughter lasts throughout life and may in colloquial terms be referred to as the most successful relationship. Mothers spend more time with their daughters than with other family members and a strong identification between mother and daughter is formed from an early age. The bond is not in any way disrupted when the daughter gets married. As we have seen, mothers-in-law take an active interest in the domestication of their daughters' husbands. The prospect of a life-long close relationship probably explains the female preference for daughters. A mother will normally lose sons when they marry, whereas a daughter may in fact enlarge the mother-in-law's dominion upon marriage.

In their early years, boys obviously identify with their mothers rather than with their fathers. At the beginning of my fieldwork I was impressed by what I took to be the masculine pose of young boys. But gradually it became clear to me that their behavior was not patterned on that of their fathers. When I became closer to a few families in the neighborhood, I recognized that the boys molded their behavior on their mothers. This could be noticed in their gestures and way of speaking, and it became clear to me that what I at first classified as exuberant, childish masculinity, was the dominant behavior of Nazarena females somehow copied by the little boys. This makes for some remarkable changes as the boys reach puberty. They of course fail to transform their childhood "masculinity" into a mature form. With the onset of puberty they somehow seem to lower their aspirations and develop the less exuberant and even sometimes resigned demeanor that is characteristic of the mature male in Nazaré. Puberty seems to be a critical and frustrating period in a Nazareno boy's life. It is not unusual that they for periods of time become morose and difficult to get along with. They suffer from impredictable moods and in periods seem to be in the grips of mild depressions. This is the time that their mothers lose interest in them and they themselves somehow understand that their behavior has to be changed—that in terms of behavior they have been betting on the wrong horse. Their situation changes when they start their careers as fishermen at 14 to 16 years of age. But it may take quite some time for them to acquire the demeanor of the grown Nazareno male.

The behavior of the mature male is, within a wide range of variation, less self-assured than that of the women. One might expect daring fishermen to behave

The boys are not allowed to go to sea before they are 14, not even for brief excursions, except for the Festival of the Sea. Going to sea under guardianship of experienced fishermen is an important and joyful event.

with a certain measure of machismo. But this trait, which is so characteristic of the Latin male, is strangely absent in Nazaré. The dominant personality trait of grown men may even be described as somewhat gentle, somewhat introverted, and sometimes resigned. This is contrary to the observations of Gilmore (1979) about the display of machismo among Spanish men. Gilmore interprets the masculine display as a kind of vicarious consummation of maleness in a system that offers few other possibilities. Gilmore's observation is probably correct, and incidentally also explains the masculine display in the urban black ghetto in the U.S. (Hannerz 1969).

The absence of this type of masculinity in Nazaré is probably due to the fulfillment of masculinity at sea. Fishing in the waters of Nazaré is dangerous, and the pursuit of fishing is to a certain degree a heroic enterprise that requires strength, persistence and daring. The cultural expectations of maleness are therefore fulfilled and do not require any measure of vicarious display.

The girls do not have the same switch in their identification as the boys. They too identify with their mothers, and some of them acquire the dominating demeanor of the Nazarena female at an early age. Some of the comparatively young girls have acquired the somewhat husky voice normally associated with masculinity. I recognized that particular huskiness whenever our neighbor gave her husband a tongue-lashing in the evening. I can still hear the somewhat deep-pitched voice of our formidable neighbor, as well as the patient and somewhat low-keyed response from her husband, when I reflect on the gender-behavior in Nazaré. Nazarena females are raised to become dominating personalities from their earliest years. They receive more attention than their brothers and have the advantage of a stable identification and the continued presence and attention of their mothers throughout their lives.

The relationship between brothers and sisters is not particularly close. The brothers do not have the same responsibility for the behavior of their sisters as is common in Mediterranean countries. In Italy brothers are the guardians of their sisters' virginity (Brøgger 1971). But then virginity does not have the same significance in Nazaré as among Italian peasants. The deflowering of their virgin brides is for Mediterranean males a symbolic act of dominance. The fathers and brothers are the custodians of this virginity in the male-dominated Mediterranean. The absence of this institution in Nazaré is probably because, given the power-relations between the sexes, the defloration of a woman does not have the same meaning as in a male dominated society. One may even be tempted to ask who is deflowering whom. Sometimes boys in their late teens will complain that they are still *virgins*. Sisters, then, do not need the protection of their brothers and, as the sure winners in the competition for their mothers' attention, they rarely develop close relationships with their brothers.

Generally speaking, a typical household does not seem to develop the kind of family affection we take for granted in middle class nuclear families. This indicates that the special affective dyadic relationships in the family are the result of a particular family structure and ideology. It is the probable outcome of what Stone (1977) has referred to as *affective individualization,* which developed with the privatization of the nuclear family. When considering the lack of intimacy in the Nazareno household it must also be taken into consideration that the house of the average family traditionally is too small to accommodate complex socializing. Also, with regard to housing, the Nazarenos to a certain degree maintain the medieval tradition.

Quite a few of the accommodations still do in fact fit Philip Ariès' (1962) description of the pre-modern houses of the common people in medieval Europe:

> They were obvious shelters for sleeping and sometimes (not always) eating. These little houses fulfilled no social function. They could not even serve as houses for families. . . . Admittedly people were not as sensitive about promiscuity under the ancien régime. But there has to be a certain amount of space, or a family life is impossible, and the concept of the family cannot take shape and develop. We may conclude that these poor, badly housed people felt a common-place love for little children—that elementary form of the concept of the family (p. 392).

Apart from the forces at play in daily routines, the cramped housing conditions of many Nazarenos in its own way hampers the development of the individualistic family.

Even nowadays when many families have acquired rather well-equipped apartments with several rooms, the situation of the males has not changed. The house is not a place for the husband to live, only to eat and sleep. Life must be lived outside. If the husband or a son hangs around the house, he will be reprimanded by the woman who wants it to be kept clean and untouchable. A commonly heard joke is about the woman who forces her husband to go to the public bath in spite of the modern bathroom they have at home.

The childhood memories of a young Nazareno from the class of fishermen may serve as a vivid illustration of the female dominance of the house:

When I was 12 years old, I went to high school. There I met new friends from the middle class. One of my closest friends was Rui. Our freedom to move around until late was a favorite subject of conversation. He was conscious that the boys of the fishing class had more freedom. I could stay till late in the evening without suffering any consequence at home. My mother wouldn't say anything about it, and my father simply didn't count. Even when I was nine years old I used to play with other boys from lower class, mostly sons of fishermen, after dinner till midnight, in the Plaza. Actually it was not possible for me or any other boy to stay at home. "The house is for the women," my mother used to say. Even when I wanted to play with other children at the door of my home, there was always a neighbor quarrelling because we were making too much noise and shouting that we should go to play on the beach like the other boys. A boy shouldn't be *econado* (from *cona,* the female reproductive organ) at home. When my sister Francelina reached 9 or 10 years she went to work in a middle class family. She had the obligation of cleaning and helping with the cooking; in return she would receive proper feeding and clothing and a small amount of money. There were various reasons for her to move out: the house was too small, and it wouldn't be proper for a girl to be sleeping near her grown-up brothers, besides, it represented a great relief for the family, since it would be a mouth less to feed.

But Nazaré today is in the process of rapid change, and it may be safely assumed that the medieval family system, which today is still common, will gradually disappear. The Nazarenos themselves are aware of the gradual transformation of family life that is taking place. Certain families will be described as modern, or by the most apt Portuguese term *aburguesado*. These modern families will be known particularly by the care they invest in their children. Children of *aburguesados* will be better groomed and dressed than the average fisherman's children, and may somewhat disparagingly be referred to as *mimoso,* spoiled. They are also subject to rigid supervision. This is particularly notable with regard to the boys of modern families. The girls were kept firmly under the control also during *l'ancien régime*. Boys of the *praia* still today enjoy a remarkable measure of freedom. Because of the dangerous conditions at sea, no boys are allowed to join their fathers on fishing till they reach 14 years of age. Thus only the school makes demands on the young boys between 7 and 14, and the average fisherman's child is not in any way expected to excel at school. A boy may even occasionally skip an entire year of schooling, and be free to enjoy his leisure.

Parental concern for scholastic performance is a certain sign of *aburguesamento*. Families who most clearly demonstrate bourgeois aspirations will in most cases have fathers who succeed in getting employment as sailors, or are unusually successful fishermen, or have mothers who are wealthy *peixeiras,* fish-sellers. The majority of the families of fishermen today belong to *l'ancien régime,* and a large percentage of their children seem prepared to follow the traditions of *gente da praia*.

3 / Manners, Behavior, and Attitudes

The difference in style of behavior between the bourgeoisie and the fishermen is striking. The demeanor of genuine Nazarenos would by most middle class Europeans be regarded as rustic, authentic, or informal, as the case may be. The term *rustic,* however, has derogatory overtones and as a term it has become obsolete because of the democratization of advanced, industrial nations. But the phenomenon is of great anthropological interest. I have therefore chosen the term "pre-bureaucratic" to describe the non-urban style of behavior that still may be observed in certain folk communities in Europe. The term is chosen not only because it is value neutral, but also because it indicates the state of organization of the community in which it commonly appears.

This behavior is characterized by a certain lack of refinement in language and body choreography, a particular authenticity in the management of encounters, a presentation of self based on the implicit, and sometimes unconscious, assumption that the audience has more or less complete knowledge of the statuses and personal resources of the actor. In encounters based on careful impression management and the mobilization of one circumscribed status, authentic behavior appears as somehow naive and innocent.

Naivety emerges only in situations in which it is contrasted with the management of behavior we refer to as formal. Formal behavior in authentic situations appears as conceited, which may be regarded as the urban counterpart to rustic naivety, both appearances reflecting a lack of cognitive appreciation of the proper definition of the situation. It is on the basis of these observations that the naive demeanor of the Nazarenos may be understood.

In its proper context, authentic behavior appears infused with commitment and participation. This is the mode of Nazareno interaction. It is never detached and formal. People communicate not only with words, but also with their bodies, emphasizing special points with expressive movements and spontaneous facial gestures. The Nazarenos themselves insist that they are full of nerves, and the style of interaction does indeed have an ethos of emotional participation. Characteristically, the women in particular will raise their voices to a high pitch even in a perfectly normal conversation. The men have less of a tendency to raise their voices and sometimes reflect on the rhetorical manners of their women, usually concluding the women's loud speech is a show of force, a theory to which I also subscribe. The women themselves are sometimes also conscious of their manners in this respect.

Their explanation is that they raise their voices because of the constant rumblings of the waves on the shores of Nazaré. This explanation, however, is shared only by the women.

Not only the rhetorical style, but also the language itself is distinctive both in phonology and semantics. Compared to the official language of Lisbon and Coïmbra it appears as lacking in phonological precision. To an outsider this lack of precision reduces the amount of information transmitted by the speaker. I never became completely familiar with the Nazareno way of speaking and had sometimes a very hard time following a running conversation between fishermen in the *tabernas*. Although I had few problems following, for example, the news broadcast from the official TV channels, I had to mobilize all my attention in order to follow a comparatively simple everyday conversation.

The effect of their pronunciation is somewhat like the experience of a telephone conversation when the quality of transmission reduces the contrast between phonemes, with a consequent fusion of closely related sounds like "p" and "b." In an English telephone conversation Benny could be confused with Penny. In order to prevent confusion over the telephone, people will sometimes emphasize a distinction with a well-known word, for example "B as in Birmingham."

What distinguishes national languages from dialects is, among other things, the emphasis on a clear and somewhat crisp pronunciation that assures a certain redundancy of phonological information. The Nazarenos appear to be cutting corners and slashing sounds here and there, transforming the phonology into a kind of stenographic minimum. This phonological economy is of course possible in a closely knit community with a high degree of shared information, and is characteristic of dialects everywhere, the degree of intelligibility somehow being dependent upon the size of its constituency.

A few examples will demonstrate the phonological habits of Nazareno fishermen.

The following expression is normally shouted when the candis-fishers (see page 86) get a particularly good catch.

Nazareno: Eh pá, barrtinhs'ó ar repá.
Standard Portuguese: Eh pá, barretinhos ao ar rapazes.

The meaning is literally translated as:

O boys, caps in the air boys.

What has been left out in the Nazareno expression is:

Eh pá barr(e)tinh(o)s (a)o ar re(a)pa(zes)

This example demonstrates the stenographic quality of their phonology: of 23 phonemes in a phrase they leave out 6, or 26 percent. In addition the initial *pá* is also a contraction of the word *rapaz,* boy, but that is common in Portuguese everywhere. The examples could be multiplied. An interested observer has in fact collected and published a great number of the linguistic demolitions perpetrated by the Nazarenos (Mactrãon 1988).

The Nazareno language is also rich in metaphors, many of which refer to experiences with fishing:

Nazareno: Fico' injoad c'm'a um carapan sec.
Standard Portuguese: Ficou enjoado como um carpau seco.

This expression refers to the reaction of someone who does not like what he hears. The literal meaning is, "He became flustered like a dry carapau." Carapau is one of the favorite species of fish, which are preserved by drying like the Norwegian bacalhao. A carapau halfway in the process of drying is commonly referred to as a *sick carapau*. (*Enjoado:* literally, *disgusted*.) Incidentally, only 17 percent of the phonemes, or 4 of 24, had been dropped in this example.

The language of the Nazarenos is closer to slang than is the norm for the national language, which in most European countries is recognized as the language of prestige, and therefore preferably spoken by the bourgeoisie. This idiomatic quality, which is characteristic both of slang and folk-language, indicates that these two forms develop under circumstances that are structurally related.

THE NAZARENO PRESENTATION OF SELF

The discourse of the Nazarenos sometimes lacks refinement in the sense that it openly alludes to areas of human life that have been tabooed by bourgeois culture.

Carapau, *one of the favorite species of fish, are preserved by drying, like the Norwegian* bacalhao. A carapau *halfway in the process of drying is commonly referred to as a* "sick carapau."

This is a most significant testimony of the fact that the Nazarenos do not share the bourgeois alienation between mind and body. Their uninhibited references to sexual and biological matters may easily shock puritan bourgeois sensibilities.

In terms of dress the Nazarenos have preserved their own regional uniforms. Although the folk costumes, which still are presented on post-cards and folk art from the village, are no longer commonly used, the Nazarenos have retained a few elements of dress that are distinct. This is particularly true of the women, who dress up in a particular style of skirt that barely reaches above the knees and is always worn with an apron. They stand out in any crowd of countrymen outside the village. This is true whether they are dressed in black, as do the widows and mourners, or in more colorful costumes. Some men still wear jackets with the checkered pattern and particular "Nazareno style" made from cloth referred to as *escosês,* Scottish.

According to local tradition this type of cloth was introduced by immigrants from Scotland who had fallen out with the powerful clans that denied commoners the use of the most appealing patterns and colors. This piece of local tradition is a reminiscence of the fact that with the rise for mercantilistic ideas in the eighteenth century foreign craftsmen were invited to settle in Portugal to promote what we today would refer to as import substituting industries, particularly in textiles and glasswork. The *escosês* cloth is also used for the trousers, *ceroulas,* which are still used by the fishermen in the upper age bracket as a kind of underwear. The cloth is particularly well adapted to the requirements of fishermen because it dries easily and keeps the body warm.

Few wear the long black caps celebrated in songs and on postcards. The common style of the first three decades of our century, today only a few old, retired fishermen can still be seen wearing them. These old caps have been replaced by the "sixpence", *boné,* which today is part of the fishermen's uniform.

On the local scene, the fishermen are easy to spot, particularly when they return from the sea in their high boots. But even when they are not dressed up for action there are no doubts about their identity. This is particularly true of the older fishermen, who still go barefoot. Their gait and their facial expressions, easier to spot than describe, also leave no doubt about their identity.

The Nazarenos are conscious of being regarded as somewhat rustic and uncouth, a fact they do not mind at all. Rather it forms the basis of a barely articulated populism that gives them a definite sense of identity. They enjoy telling stories of how Nazarenos shock the polite society with their loud voices, rude manners, and particularly colorful use of the Portuguese language.

The fishermen have nothing of the somewhat humble style that is often found among peasants, and which testifies to centuries of oppression and exploitation by the landed gentry. The fishermen present themselves as independent, but without any arrogance or swaggering pride. Rather they may sometimes appear somewhat morose, and not particularly keen to make a friendly impression. This is especially true of older men.

The women display more self-confidence and pride in their presentation of self than do the men. They walk with a self-assured gait that makes their dress move from side to side in a rhythmic way, and which gives the impression that the movements are carefully choreographed. Particularly when they carry heavy loads on their heads, they make an impressive sight.

THE HISTORICAL CONTEXT OF MANNERS AND ATTITUDES

Social historians have given us some clues to the circumstances in which private life emerged from the teeming communality of medieval society (Flandrin 1976; Ariès 1962). The phenomenon of privacy is inextricably linked to certain architectural developments in the design of living quarters, as pointed out earlier.

Until the end of the seventeenth century, private quarters were not developed.

> . . . there were still large rooms, opening into each other: people slept, ate, and lived in them amid the coming and going of servants, children, and visitors, the servants not hesitating more than the children to take part in the conversation of their masters and the latter's friends, if one is to believe the evidence of the *Caquets de l'Accouchée* or the comedies of Moliére. At night the servants slept near their masters, often in the same room, ready to answer their summons. (Flandrin 1979, p. 93)

At all times privacy was unknown; each person, according to Jean Louis Flandrin, lived in a state resembling the court at Versailles. However,

> In the eighteenth century, however, corridors were introduced, and had the effect of giving autonomy to the rooms, which became specialized, more numerous and individual. The ladies, during the day, could shut themselves up in their boudoirs, or receive their close friends in small drawing-rooms. The servants were driven back to the kitchen, the servants' hall, and the antechambers, and attempts were made to prevent the children from being too familiar with them. Within the confines of the great households, the modern family began to achieve its independence. (Flandrin 1979, p. 93)

The privatization of family life was just the beginning of a process of compartmentalization of social life that followed in the wake of bureaucratization, industrialization, urbanization, and social stratification. With this development of exclusive and segregated arenas followed a transformation of the style of interaction and presentation of self.

The American anthropologist Erving Goffman has demonstrated how human behavior can be understood as a kind of theatrical performance. Human beings are really actors who try to mold their behavior in accordance with social situations. Sometimes they try to hide information that may damage their performance, and sometimes they may even try to deceive their audience. With this perspective in mind, the difference between the folk community and the urban society becomes particularly important. The scope for deception is much larger in the urban society than in the folk community where everybody knows one another from childhood. In the context of the big city, a formal code is developed as a way to control and structure information. A formal code of behavior will tend to emerge when knowledge from different arenas of the life of an individual is compartmentalized. With the management of social relationships within these structures, a new understanding of social life becomes possible. The more or less conscious manipulation of information that is required when both arenas and audiences are shifting sharpens the sensitivity to the make-believe quality of social life.

Different parts of the self are parcelled out, and different parts are presented in mutually exclusive arenas. This sharpens the sensitivity to the amount of acting involved in the presentation of self. The necessity of distinguishing between different codes and situations requires the development of new cognitive categories, for example "private" and "public," as well as a more conscious idea of the self as an independently acting agent in human encounters. Of particular importance for modern human beings is the division into the private *backstage* and the public *front stage*. Backstage, secluded from the world at large, human beings prepare themselves for the act on the front stage and also relax from the strains of public or communal participation (see page 61).

With the development of a sensitivity to cope with different situations, personal behavior out of necessity becomes less spontaneous and more calculated. A certain measure of objectivity must be developed, particularly with regard to the self. In order to adapt to different situations, an ability to view the self from outside is necessary. As the folk community gives way to urban forms, a different type of personality is developed and a comparatively rural innocence gives way to an urban sophistication.

It is understood that out of necessity social situations are constructs based on the mastery of codes and the manipulation of information. When we know that behind the masks we present in a social situation a different reality may exist, we may develop a measure of cynicism. This is particularly the case when we know that most people have skeletons in the closet. But instead of cynicism we may acquire a deeper understanding of human nature and social life.

Parallel to these developments, in recent European history, a new moralism became evident, mainly as a repercussion of the Protestant Reformation. The most articulate version of this moralistic ethos is found in the Reformed Protestantism of Calvin's Geneva. Not only was a sterner conception of sin developed, but we also see evidence in the public conscience of a new attitude to the physical nature of man. The hallmark of this attitude was an intellectualism that demanded a suppression of human passions and the simpler expressions of man's animal nature. A new code of behavior requiring the strictest control of man's physical nature emerged, and the restricted code of bourgeois politeness was created.

Seen from the point of view of this puritanical ethos, the communal and intimate nature of social life that preceded this revolution in mores seems disgusting. As Flandrin (1976) reminds us,

> We reject the communal living of former times less out of virtue than by reason of an instinctive repugnance. We admit sexual contacts only with selected persons. The warmth and odor of another person, when they do not attract us, provoke our aversion. Is it due to a refinement of our sensibility, or our modesty, that is the integration, at the most profound level, of taboos of which we are hardly conscious? It is in any case remarkable that in tracing the history of family feeling, it is usually only those aspects of the communal living of former times that may run counter to our own family sentiments—the throwing open of the house, the room and even the bed to strangers—that have been emphasized. It has not occurred to historians to see in this practice one of the bases of the cohesion of the family in past times. There is, in our present-day delicacy, a sort of neurotic individualism that militates against the spontaneity of our relations with other people and perhaps with the members of our reduced family. (p. 100)

The two forces, the more complex social structure (partly reflected in architecture) and the breakthrough of puritanism, created together a new style of behavior that we refer to as bourgeois. This style of behavior, which started as a phenomenon of the elite, gradually gained ground in the centuries that followed. With regional variations, this style is typical of the Western bourgeois culture and is today in the process of becoming, in a somewhat diluted form, standard European behavior.

One of the "evils" cogently fought by the moralists of the sixteenth and seventeenth centuries was the custom of the whole family, including the servants, to sleep in the same bed. Thus the Bishop of Grenoble, Msgr Camus, wrote in 1681: "We have ascertained in the course of our visits that one of the means which the devil most commonly uses to make children lose their purity of soul by depriving them of that of the body, is the custom of many fathers and mothers of having their children sleep in the same bed with them . . . when they are beginning to have the use of reason." He therefore ordered the parish priest to make every effort "to remedy an evil so prevalent and so detrimental to the salvation of souls" (Flandrin 1976, p.99).

The years in which the great transformation of community life took place, starting with the sixteenth century, was also the period of the great moralists, first among the Protestants, and somewhat later among the Catholics. This was the period when the nuclear family gradually retreated from the conviviality of the common rooms, and servants withdrew to the kitchen; and the separation was not only between social classes, but also between grown-ups and children. The moralists of this period were the architects of the modern and the neurotic personality of our time. The obsession of these generations of moralists with moral purity in a sense reflects the great process of separation between social classes and social situations.

The animal nature of man posed in opposition to the spiritual realm probably served as a meaningful idiom for the dominant themes in social development: the compartmentalization of social life and the refinement of manners. If this is the case, then the compartmentalization of social life, the breakdown of the medieval community, and the moral frenzy of the spiritual elite are part of the same process of social development. The moral frenzy of the spiritual elite refers to the strong condemnation of moral shortcomings that became part of Protestant, and particularly Calvinist, teaching. Particularly condemned were the sins of the flesh, but generally speaking the animal nature or non-spiritual qualities in the human soul became the target of moral condemnation. Human beings, it was argued, should be clean in word and deed, and develop an iron self-control in order to control human passions.

Social historians have recently traced this development as it appears in the pictographic annals, contemporary descriptions, diaries, codes of behavior, manuals for confessors, and moralistic pamphlets (Flandrin 1976; Shorter 1975; Stone 1977; Ariès 1962). As in the case of the developmental history of the family, this knowledge of the development of the human personality gives our observations of the rapidly dwindling folk societies of our time a new frame of reference. It forces the anthropologist out of a synchronic frame of mind and makes apparently insignificant observations of behavior important data for a broader understanding of the development of the human personality.

ATTITUDES TOWARD CHILDREN AND SEX

When a Nazareno father complains that he has to share the conjugal bed with his children, however, he is not echoing the concern of the Bishop of Grenoble, but rather expressing a certain envy of people with less cramped living-space. Obviously this Narareno father, as far as household arrangements are concerned, shares important features with his predecessor in the sixteenth century. This observation inspires the assumption that the rustic behavior of the Nazarenos represents a continuation of medieval ways, and indicates that this community of fishermen has not been subject to the great bourgeois transformation of the preceding centuries.

It is not only the communal nature of social life that indicates the preservation of archaic forms in the village, but also Nazareno attitudes toward sex and the physical nature of humans. An observation of Ariès (1962) is of particular interest in this connection:

> One of the unwritten laws of contemporary morality, the strictest and best respected of all, requires adults to avoid any reference, above all any humorous reference, to sexual matters in the presence of children. This notion was entirely foreign to the society of old. The modern reader of the diary in which Henry IV's physician, Heroard, recorded the details of the young Louis XIII's life is astonished by the liberties people took with their children, by the coarseness of the jokes they made, and by the indecency of gestures made in public which shocked nobody and which was regarded as perfectly natural. (p. 100)

The Nazarenos have what an enlightened modernist would refer to as a healthy attitude toward sex. They have not been persuaded that sex is particularly sinful and do not observe the modern taboo of refraining from referring to sex in the presence of children. My first encounter with this unadulterated attitude to sexual matters took place when I was served a cup of wine in a kitchen crowded with men, women, and children. As I drank the cup, a red phallus appeared fixed to the bottom. My surprise was received with a noisy display of mirth both among the grown-ups and the children. Sex jokes will also be told in the presence of children, who obviously are not ashamed to enjoy them.

Once a grandfather brought his little grandson with him to a *taberna,* and he asked the child to sing a song, which the boy did:

Ah Maria
se queres que a menina cresça
com água da cona
lava-lhe a cabeça

Oh Mary
if you want the child to grow
wash the head
with water from the vagina.

This phallic reference to the act of conception was favorably received. A woman who was working in the *taberna,* however, good-naturedly reproached him with the words, "The grandfather is worse than the child."

The ribaldry of the society of fishermen once provoked a dramatic encounter with the authorities at the end of the Carnival. According to local custom, the Carnival is ended with the funeral of a mock saint, *Santo Entrudo*. An effigy of the saint is made of straw and paraded through the streets. Behind the saint a group of young men dressed up in black as widows serve as the so-called *carpideiras,* professional wailers hired for funerals. They solemnly proceed with a loud measure of mock wailing.

One year a big carrot was placed at the crotch of the effigy as a big erect penis, a display that the audience received with loud cries of amused appreciation. The police, however, intervened and tried to stop the procession. The Nazarenos refused to remove the carrot and asked the police if they did not have one themselves. The police defended their interference with reference to the many children present, thus demonstrating a typical bourgeois attitude. The women laughed at this prudery, shouting that little boys knew that they had a thing between their legs and that even the little girls knew, too. *(Os meninos sabem que têm una coisinha entre as pernas, e as meninas também.)* It is notable that the ribaldry of the women is worse than that of the men. The most popular word of impatient exclamation among the women is *caralho* (penis).

The local producer of china caters to what amounts to a jokingly framed cult of the phallus with a production of an assortment of erotic artifacts, the most popular of which is an enormous, red phallus. These artifacts, however, are kept hidden and will be displayed only on special occasions, the favorite of which is the Carnival.

NAZARENOS AND PURITANISM

It is a general observation that the Nazarenos do not demonstrate the kind of inhibitions that today have become second nature to the European middle class. As Norbert Elias (1936) reminds us, these inhibitions are the result of what he refers to as the civilizing process. The gradual process of refinement of behavior, from table manners to speech, hits with particular severity the expression of the grosser biological aspects of human activity. As Berger and Berger (1983) point out, all purely organic expressions have been subject to this process, but the sexual and gastrointestinal system of the human organism have been especially important targets.

As already observed, this process of refinement is but one aspect of the transformation of human behavior that followed in the wake of the Reformation, both the Protestant and the Catholic. As examples of a prebureaucratic style of behavior, the Nazareno case is of particular interest both from a cultural anthropological and a psychological perspective. It confirms a general observation to the effect that the puritan ethos of the moralist reformers of the sixteenth and seventeenth centuries struck deeper roots in Protestant than in Catholic communities. The reason for this seems to be partly that puritan spirit was both less severe and less common among the Catholic clergy than among the Protestant.

Puritanism in the widest sense of the word was at the heart of the Protestant Reformation and it became party to popular movements that were widespread in the

years following the emancipation of northern Europe from the Roman Catholic
Church. The spiritual monopoly of the Catholic clergy prevented the popular spread
of puritanism in southern Europe. Although Nazaré may not be representative of
Mediterranean folk communities, it is probably true that the puritan transformation
of behavior had less effect in southern than in northern Europe. The common notion
that southern Europeans tend to be more spontaneous and open than northerners is
not without foundation. The difference reflects the emphasis on personal and
individual control which was demanded by the Protestant evangelists. Some critics
of Calvin have accused him of a desire to turn the whole society into a Benedictine
monastery. The lay people in the Roman Catholic Church were not expected to be
perfect; extreme virtue was merely expected of the saints and the religious specialists. Ordinary people were expected to be sinners dependent for their salvation on
the indulgence of the Church through the sacrament of confession. Calvin, by
abolishing indulgence and religious virtuosos like saints and religious specialists,
democratized virtue.

At the same time Calvin preached the idea of predestination. According to his
idea there was nothing the individual human being could do to promote his own
salvation. God's grace alone decided who would be damned or who would be
granted eternal life in heaven. Moreover, it had all been decided beforehand. Your
own conduct could not in any way change your prospects. A commonsensical
conclusion would have been to forego all inhibitions and seek as much enjoyment as
possible in this world. But confronted with the grave uncertainty with regard to
destiny, human psychology proved to be much more sophisticated. The crucial
question became: Am I among the saved? Faced with this uncertainty, the diagnosis
of grace emerged as the existential question above all others. Cleanliness in word
and deed became the crucial diagnostic sign of grace. Even if willpower by no
means could alter the state of grace, human beings chose to struggle hard to mold
their thoughts and conduct in accordance with the diagnostic optimum. In a way
they did not give up the idea of influencing destiny through their style of life and
thinking. Who could tell whether an exemplary life was the result of willpower or a
diagnostic sign of being chosen? A desire and struggle for a virtuous life indeed
could be conceived as the redeeming diagnostic sign. To have success as a thrifty
laborer in God's vineyard was also regarded as a favorable diagnostic sign. As the
German sociologist Max Weber has pointed out, this belief is at the heart of what he
referred to as the spirit of capitalism. If a person through skill, thrift, and frugality
acquired a fortune, that was a favorable indicator of grace. This complex of ideas
not only promoted a spirit of both economic and spiritual individualism, but
fostered a transformation of consciousness and manner of being.

When the idea of cleanliness became the dominant metaphor of ethical judgment, not only dirt in the spiritual sense, but also in the cruder physical form
became a crucial concern. The psychological consequences of this complex of ideas
was a repression of sinful thoughts and struggle against dirt and disorders in any
conceivable form. This spiritual regime fostered the modern northern European, a
human being with a high measure of self-control, and one not favorably disposed
towards wordly enjoyments.

Centuries later the psychological consequences of this puritan ethos was to be the main focus of Sigmund Freud's investigation of the human mind. He demonstrated that repression of basic human motives like the sex-drive was detrimental to general well-being and sometimes caused not only physical symptoms, but also extreme mental distress. Historically, psychoanalysis appears to be a rational way of coping with the distress caused by the repression of the animal nature of human beings. As far as the psychoanalytic conception of mental health is concerned, the Nazarenos appear as less neurotic than the average northern European or American, if "neurotic" is meant to refer to a mental state impressed by fears of losing a strict control of impulses and a consequent difficulty of spontaneous, social participation. The Nazarenos in this sense appear less neurotic indeed than the average northern European or American, both of whom are especially concerned with cleanliness and order. In fact this concern may be even stronger in the USA, where it is sometimes manifested in crusading movements against social phenomena that offend the puritan sensibility. Because the USA was for centuries the principal haven of puritan immigrants, this seems quite natural. In the USA we still find utopian Protestant communities, like the Amish and the Mennonites, which no longer exist in Europe.

It would be most unfair to maintain that the Nazarenos lack a sense of cleanliness. Washing, both of houses and clothes, is one of the principal activities of women. What is absent is the generalized concern for cleanliness and order in the widest sense which is typical of the puritans. The Nazarenos are tolerant of people who do not conform; they are not afraid of coloring their language with reference to sex and bodily functions and may give in to their emotions more readily than the average European or American bourgeois.

CHILD TRAINING

As pointed out by Berger and Berger (1983), the hallmarks of bourgeois mentality have been most adequately summarized by Benjamin Franklin as frugality, enterprise, decency, common sense, abstinence, discipline, reliability, politeness, respect, and fairness. To train children to conform to these lofty characteristics is an awesome task indeed. As was clear to pedagogues from the heroic age of bourgeois culture, this could not be left entirely to parents, but required the professional assistance of school and church. But the parents were expected to be the main promoters of the transformation of a child into a useful bourgeois citizen. The history of the rise of bourgeois culture therefore is also the history of the domestication of the child.

In order to develop into wholesome citizens, the children of the heroic age of bourgeois culture became subject to a rigid program of training that above all emphasized discipline and cleanliness in word and deed. In their appreciation of the nature of the child, the Calvinists particularly emphasized Original Sin. In order to save the child from this legacy of the expulsion from the Garden of Eden, the children should be subjected to a ruthless suppression. It was therefore the duty of teachers and parents to beat discipline and sense into the younger generation. This rigid treatment had as its goal the austere individualist striving for perfection. The unifying idea was personal control and self-assurance. This primarily Protestant idea of "personhood" is responsible for the authentic bourgeois who maintains a pronounced sense of individual responsibility and personal control of the self (as well as circumstances) and has a strong sense of duty and thrift.

The pedagogic regime geared to this idea of personhood did indeed succeed in creating this awesome hero of the rising bourgeoisie of the seventeenth and eighteenth centuries. It should also be mentioned that the personal cost, in terms of psychic agony which this regime exacted, is no less awesome than Sigmund Freud demonstrated in his study of the *Culture and Its Discontent* (1930). That this was the price that had to be paid for the rise of modern capitalism has been demonstrated by Max Weber in *The Protestant Ethic and the Spirit of Capitalism* (1904–5).

The Catholic laymen were spared the trials and tribulations of the Protestant bourgeois elite, which was reflected not only in a slower economic growth, but also in a maintenance of a less individualistic and less tormented model of personality. The austere discipline of the Catholic counter-reformation was primarily shouldered by the religious elites, like the Jesuits, and did not become the ideal for the Catholic laymen. This is one of the main reasons for the less rigid claims of puritanism in Catholic countries. It accounts for the less punitive spirit and the higher measure of tolerance for human shortcomings that is found in southern European folk communities, of which Nazaré is probably a characteristic example.

The Nazarenos do not share the lofty ideals the bourgeois culture holds for its children. Fishermen's children therefore are not subject to the same form of domestication as those of the bourgeoisie. This can readily be observed among the few *aburguesado* children from the class of fishermen. These well-groomed boys and girls are a frequent subject of derision among the more uncouth and free-wheeling children of *gente da praia*. As mentioned, the modern families in Nazaré will be known particularly by the care they invest in their children. The average Nazarenos do not expect their children to succeed in the competitive bourgeois society and therefore do not breed into them the tireless ambition we know in latter-day northern European puritanism. They are therefore spared what Arnold Gehlen (1980) has called the "loss of naturalness" (p. 38) that bourgeois culture, with its strong emphasis on rationalism, demands from its children. They are less subjected to conscious efforts to mold their personalities and therefore rarely subject to a regimentation of austere discipline.

If the Nazarenos are harsh with their children, it is momentary, and not part of a conscious pedagogic strategy. They may occasionally beat their children, but are unable to sustain the sight of a suffering child as soon as the heat of their temper has passed. They may therefore almost immediately comfort their children with a lavish display of affection in the same sweep of behavior that triggered their aggression. Child rearing is not regarded as an art or a science that demands their special attention, but is part of the general management of daily chores. The children are therefore given a generous measure of freedom from adult supervision.

Because of their marginal status within the household, fathers do not maintain an intimate supervision of the behavior of their children. Thus, left to the care of mothers who usually are too busy with their engagements in their separate gender-culture to be overly concerned with them, the children are rarely subjected to anxious parental concern. But this lack of minute monitoring is made up for by a general warmheartedness. A Nazareno child seldom has reason to feel unwanted. On the other hand, they fail to develop that particular form of disciplined strength of character demanded by bourgeois culture. This is part of the explanation for the lack of social mobility among the class of the fishermen. Most fishermen feel distinctly uncomfortable in bourgeois company, a fact that accounts for an almost perfect apartheid between *pé calçado* and *gente da praia*. A fisherman will avoid the cafés and restaurants of the middle class and stubbornly stick to his own *taberna*.

Although some bourgeois training is offered the children at school, few children of the fishermen's class take advantage of it. They normally drop out of school after having completed the obligatory six years, which in many cases does not make them more than half literate. Most of the women over forty did not get any schooling at all, and are therefore in most cases, despite their dominant position in the family, completely illiterate. The school system, although open to all without charge, is still predominantly patronized by middle class children. The few gifted children of the class of fishermen who excel at school, have, in spite of their gifts, difficulties in adapting to the bourgeois culture. These difficulties do not relate to what we may refer to as technological proficiency, but to a failure to develop the particular middle class mentality that today is part of bourgeois culture also in Catholic countries.

It appears that the family today is still the crucial institution in the formation of personality and attitudes. The difference between the folk culture of Nazaré and the bourgeoisie is more pronounced than the difference between the working class and the bourgeoisie in northern Europe, and the chasm that separates them is not easily bridged. Not even superior intellectual gifts are sufficient to conquer the nagging sense of inferiority and alienation experienced by the few who have made it. It appears that the folk culture of Nazaré, with its strong communal character and archaic forms, leaves its children with a consciousness that is similar to an ethnic identity, and which demands almost an act of conversion to release its grip.

The strength of the folk culture of Nazaré, however, is not only felt in what it fails to deliver, but also in terms of what it offers. This will be explored in a later chapter.

DEFINITIONS OF PERSONHOOD IN NAZARÉ

On page 49 it was explained why a formal code tends to develop in an urban setting. There is little polite formalism seen in the Nazareno style of interaction. They approach each other as if they have more or less complete knowledge of each other. With some reservations this may be close to the truth. Because not even the house constitutes a secluded arena, complete privacy is rare and more or less restricted to fleeting, intimate encounters. It is this lack of mutually exclusive arenas that is the hallmark of the folk community. The communality of the traditional medieval village prevailed precisely because of the lack of privacy. A villager will usually be closely identified with his village. The good news about the village is that it does not breed loneliness and alienation. The bad news is that it fosters a parochial mentality in the widest sense of the word. It is parochial because the more abstract relationships on which the modern national state is based have little appeal to villagers. It is parochial also because there are practically no specialized arenas where different styles of life may be developed. Consequently people have to be more average than in an urban setting.

Not unexpectedly, a visible gay lifestyle cannot be found in Nazaré, although the identity of practicing homosexuals seems to be generally known. Homosexuals in Nazaré referred to as *paneleiros,* are regarded as deviants. Either they have to adapt their lifestyle to the common average or remain marginal. But then again, being marginal in Nazaré is not the same as being marginal in a community of puritans, who have often persecuted homosexuals, sometimes even burning them at the stake. The Nazarenos neither persecute their homosexuals nor condemn them. But they are the objects of a number of clever jokes, usually behind their backs. This makes it somewhat difficult to have a serious discussion of the issue as such, because there is a general unwillingness to talk about *paneleiros* in anything but jocular terms. A puritan will also be surprised to find that it is not considered damaging to male self-respect to have a relationship with a *paneleiro,* provided it is as the active partner. This attitude, however, applies to the folk community of fishermen and does not seem to be shared by the bourgeois stratum.

Most Nazarenos of the fishermen's class feel that their status as Portuguese citizens is less significant than their status as *gente da praia.* They regard both the bureaucratic state and the bourgeois society as somewhat alien. Their basic identity is achieved through their membership in the Nazareno community. Although a measure of political consciousness has emerged through the establishment of parliamentary democracy, it is still true that the civic status implied in the modern concept of citizen cannot be meaningfully achieved by most Nazarenos.

Precisely because of the humane qualities of their community, the bureaucratic definition of personhood is unsatisfactory. This explains why practically all Nazarenos are known by their own nicknames or that of their family. The nicknames sometimes refer to personal traits, sometimes to particular events or conditions. Nicknames are felt to be expressive of the unique personal status of an individual, whereas the official name is associated with a somewhat alien world. Nicknaming possibly duplicates the original process of naming before the bureaucratic state froze the corpus of name and thus divorced the system of person identification from its creative social context. Several of the official names held by Nazaré fishermen—like *Robalo* (a particularly expensive fish), *Borda d'Água* (seashore), *Casalinho* (small house)—obviously originated as nicknames. This is true also for other Mediterranean communities. The origin of many official names in, for example, Italy can no longer be ascertained, but a significant number still have that personal ring of authentic nicknames, often with humorous, sometimes slightly malicious allusions, that reveal their idiosyncratic nature (for example *Indelicato* and *Piccolo,* small; and *della Horta,* from the garden.

Many nicknames in Nazaré reveal not only an anti-bureaucratic attitude toward person definition, but also reflect the Nazareno linguistic ribaldry. Names like *Pé Cagado* (shitty foot) and *Caga-à-rola* (shitting in a ring) are somewhat shocking to middle-class sensitivity. These names are also quite clearly of an anti-heroic nature. Compared to American Indian names like Shaking Thunder and Great Buffalo,

The fishermen are easier to spot than to describe. This face will be recognized by most Portugese as an authentic man of the praia.

Portuguese as well as Italian nicknames sound profane indeed. The comparison may seen far fetched, but it is relevant because in a most picturesque way it expresses the differing ethos of Indian tribes and European folk communities. The highsounding Indian names capture the spirit of the warrior and have a certain similarity to the names of the European feudal nobility, like Richard the

Lionhearted. Nazareno nicknames seem to express in their own special way the spirit of an egalitarian community.

As such, nicknames are in tune with the style of joking relationships to which the Nazarenos are particularly prone. As we know from the celebrated paper by Radcliff-Brown (1952), joking relationships may be regarded as a peaceful accommodation to latent conflicts. As we shall see in a different chapter, social life in Nazaré is fraught with conflicts that frequently erupt into the open. These conflicts, which probably are endemic to egalitarian communities, relate to the conflict between the incompatible values of equality and excellence. In peasant societies this conflict may be muted by rituals of redistribution and communality and a deliberate downplay of all symbols of success and achievement. In Nazaré the social organization of fishing is based on an individualism unmitigated by any institution of sharing and cooperation and results in enormous differences in wealth and prosperity. The institution of nicknaming may in fact be regarded as one of the mechanisms through which the Nazarenos maintain symbolic equality. Through nicknames like *Raba Coelho* (rabbit's tail), *Alhina* (small eye), and *Tomé da Bota* (Thomas of the boots), rich and successful fishing entrepreneurs are kept within an egalitarian frame of reference and discouraged from attempts towards social differentiation.

The individualization of person definition that the Nazarenos share with both Indian tribes and feudal nobility has as its opposite number the bureaucratization of names through which person definition is removed from its creative context and forced into a frame of colorless abstraction. The social correlate to this mode of classification is the official arena defined by the bureaucratic state, which does not allow for idiosyncratic personal qualities. This is in tune with the bureaucratic ethos, which prefers a homogenized mass to a community of individuals. The bureaucratic procedure of naming therefore can be regarded as part of a power strategy through which individuals are kept in their place and made more easy to govern. The bureaucratic corpus of names then serves as a linguistic uniform, a "grey flannel suit" that deprives the holder of any measure of personal distinction and only allows for completely arbitrary combinations of morphemes to keep one person apart from the other.

From this perspective the nicknaming in Nazaré may appear as a revolt against the bureaucratization of names. But that would be overlooking its origin as an older system of person definition. That the process of nicknaming is very much alive in Nazaré is therefore another indication that the community of Nazarenos has not been conquered by bourgeois culture, but has retained a prebureaucratic communal character, more characteristic of medieval times than of the twentieth century.

THE STRESS AND MANAGEMENT OF COMMUNAL LIVING

As we have seen, one of the main characteristics of the communal life in Nazaré is the lack of privacy. Not that everyone has access to your home, but enough people will normally be present to prevent it from becoming a place of seclusion for its members. Husband and wife moreover orient their lives more towards their own peer groups than toward each other.

Besides, an important locus of domestic life is played out in the entrance to the house and the street outside, or for the more privileged, the patio. A family cannot retreat into privacy without raising criticism and suspicion. People are not expected to have a private, or as it appears to the Nazarenos, a secret life. Your door should be open, and if not, you run the risk of being regarded as a witch. This happened to an elderly lady who lived by herself. Rumors were circulating to the effect that she consorted with the devil. According to one story, she was surprised by two women when she was having intercourse with the devil. She was often blamed for unexplained misfortune. Fishermen engaged in *bacalhau* fishing on the Newfoundland banks reported that they had actually seen her silhouette one foggy evening. This not only demonstrates the atmosphere created by communal living, but also indicates that the classical European ideas of witchcraft and sorcery are still alive in Nazaré.

Because Nazarenos rarely experience the privilege of withdrawing into an inaccessible world of privacy, they are of course unaware of what they are missing. Yet they obviously enjoy situations in which they can escape the pressures of the all-embracing community. One of the favorite pastimes of the more affluent fishermen is to make excursions to villages in the rural hinterland of Nazaré. To depart from Nazaré with a small group of friends to one of the insignificant rural settlements creates a sense of freedom that provokes a Dionysian frame of mind among the participants. (Consult map on page 10.)

Excursions to the sleepy hollow of Maiorga which it sometimes was my priviledge to attend was undertaken with a level of excitement that could not have been more boisterous and filled with glee if it had been to one of the more notorious areas in swinging Amsterdam or Bangkok. In order to truly appreciate an outing of this nature, a thorough exposure to the ever-present scrutiny of fellow villagers must have been endured.

In spite of my struggle to be a true participant with a full commitment to the communal life of Nazaré, I did not have the same feeling of release as my companions when leaving the scrutiny of fellow Nazarenos behind at our excursions. This lack of ability to completely relax and participate when outside the censorship of the local community was possibly due to my puritan background as a northern European. I was restrained by an ever-present Freudian censor inside me, not by real human beings in the local community. This experience more than any other made the difference between the northerners and southerners clear to me. The northerners have been released from the pressures of communal living but have not gained a true freedom, having substituted the pressure of the community with an internalized censor that can never be left behind.

Another way of escaping from the ever-present reality of the community is through heavy drinking. People drink for various reasons, but in a community like Nazaré, drink seems to promote a change in what one is tempted to call ritual status. A man who is drunk in Nazaré is shedding part of his everyday identity and enters a state in which he may resort to behavior that normally would not be tolerated. When in an intoxicated state, a man is granted a certain measure of immunity. What is said and done while in this state is not subjected to normal sanctions.

António Rui, a young fisherman of 24, got drunk one evening and started to boast:

There are no men of the *praia* who are as clever as me at sea. You can ask my uncle António who is a master. He has a very high regard of me, and would never go to sea if I were not with him. I am like a God for him. I am always working very hard. That is my defect *(o meu mal)*. I always concentrate on my work. Therefore I fail to observe the landmarks *(sinais de terra)*. That is my misfortune *(pouca sorte)*. I wish I was less dexterous and more lazy, then I could observe the landmarks and know our position. Because of this I don't feel safe enough to get my own boat, and that prevents me from becoming a great master. The others of my age are not worth more than me, but in spite of this I am not able to make a better impression than they do. But they have luck *(sorte)*. Sometimes I think that these fellows are not worth much, but they have so much luck that I want to cry.

These confessions were quite pathetic. But because of his intoxication, he was not taken seriously. In that moment, the encounter on the *taberna* served him as a session of group therapy. He could expose his lonely daydreams without the risk that his confessions would be turned against him at a later date. Through heavy drinking, a ritual form of privacy is created that guarantees a measure of discretion. The guarantee, however, is based on the belief that a man who is drunk is not really himself. Thus, even if his confessions should become common knowledge, it does not reflect on his normal self. Although it may seem strange from a conventional point of view, drunken encounters in the *taberna* are somewhat similar to public confessions as practiced by religious sects, such as the Lestadians of northern Scandinavia. Just as the prayer hall creates a privileged space in which the soul can be purged through confession without being subject to normal sanctions, the *tabernas* become ritual arenas.

This fact explains why the fishermen are suspicious of people who refuse to drink. These fail in a way to participate in the ritual and thus may appear as threatening outsiders and informers. By getting drunk you demonstrate your confidence, shed the armor and put weapons aside. In order to be accepted by the community of fishermen, it seems necessary at least on certain occasions to get properly drunk and, preferably, demonstrate your vulnerability either in word or deed. It was my good fortune in spite of my puritan background to destroy the neon light in a basement *taberna* in a somewhat Dionysian display of Norwegian dance. The bacchanal of that evening served as an efficient ritual of initiation.

CARNIVAL

A similar opportunity to act out in a ritually protected arena is offered by Carnival. This explains at least some of the enormous enthusiasm in which *Carnaval* is celebrated in Nazaré. During the Carnival Festival, any behavior, within reasonable limits, is regarded as legitimate and not to be taken seriously.

Carnival is no doubt the single most important communal event of the year. It mobilizes popular attention much more intensely than Christmas. This is at least partly because the main theme of Carnival is a play with identities, where people are invited to embrace mock identities and are thereby released from their regular, monolithic selves, the daily burden of communal living.

Carnival, which precedes Lent, a period of fasting before Easter, obviously is the continuation of a pagan ritual made slightly more acceptable to the sensibility of the clergy when presented as a preparation for the fast. The folk-etymological interpretation of its name as related to *carne,* meat, is generally accepted at the cost of the more likely interpretation that it is the continuation of the Roman ritual of Carro Navale. It has retained much of its character of saturnalia, permitting things normally prohibited, such as the exchange of roles between men and women.

The organization of the Carnival is along lines long established by tradition. Therefore it does not merit detailed description apart from elements that are distinctly Nazareno. One of these features is the degree of popular participation. Only the old and sick do not participate actively, and much time and effort is spent on the preparation of disguises, which is the essence of Carnival in Nazaré. Even households with very limited means will allocate scarce resources so as to be able to participate even if they have to strain their credit close to its limits.

The major event of Carnival is the public balls. Although arranged by the business class in Nazaré for profit, they are perceived as genuinely Nazareno. These balls, which last for four nights, starting in the evening and lasting into the sunrise, are the main arena for the display of the various disguises. At the same time these balls are an occasion for the bands in Nazaré to demonstrate their high standard of musicianship. A year's Carnival will have its own tunes and lyrics in a traditional style, and these become the musical emblems of that particular year.

Carnival, the event of the year in Nazaré, offers a release from the strains of communal living. The play with bogus identities promotes an atmosphere of license and mobilizes satiric talents.

Although the dances always start with individual couples dancing in the European ballroom tradition, from the crowded chaos on the floor dancers materialize in circles and strings in an unorganized and spontaneous move toward a pattern of folkdance. These improvised structures of dancers apparently emerge because people from the same neighborhood tend to gravitate together around a nucleus of women. A person adopted by a circle of this nature will become part of a group that during intervals will withdraw to smaller parties in the homes of the participants. Alcohol, refreshments, and cakes will be served, and the high spirits are kept up by horseplay and singing, the party gradually ambulating between the houses.

Carnival creates an intoxicating atmosphere, the nature of which is hard to describe. But anyone who has experienced communal rituals should be able to imagine the particular inner joy that becomes associated with its symbols, music, and scenarios. The emblematic marches composed by Nazareno composers will recall that particular nostalgic glow created by the unique chemistry of carnivalesque fellowship. Although the explicit ethos of Carnival is to explode or turn loose *(de arrebentar),* it serves to crystallize a spirit of unity that in the humdrum of everyday life is experienced at a much lower temperature.

Although a carnival may be organized in a grand style in big alienated cities with a great show of pomp and music, the particular spirit of fellowship that makes the Carnival into the greatest experience of the year, requires a true *folk community.* The great feeling of release can only be experienced on the background of a close-knit community in which people are unable to withdraw into a stable, secluded privacy apart from the all-embracing community. This explains why the bourgeoisie more or less appear as bystanders on this great event of *gente da praia.*

4 / Supernatural Affliction and the Structures of Relationships

In the preceding chapter we have seen how manners, behavior and attitudes in Nazaré relate to the communal nature of the community. This fact is crucial to an understanding of prebureaucratic culture. The European folk community is above all characterized by communal living, ascribed relationships, and a comparatively rudimentary differentiation of social groups, arenas of interaction, and social roles. As we have seen, prebureaucratic manners, behavior, and attitudes clearly relate to these dimensions of the social structure.

In the following we shall explore an aspect of Nazareno culture that most people clearly will recognize as premodern: the belief in supernatural affliction. After a general discussion of the relationship between the interpretation of disease and misfortune and social structure, we shall proceed with the Nazareno case with particular attention to the structure of the relationships.

As shown by Murdock (1980) in his last contribution to comparative ethnography, practically speaking every culture that may be described as premodern entertains theories of the supernatural causation of disease and misfortune. These theories may be classified either as theories of mystical, animistic, or magical causation. Of the three, the theories of mystical causation may be regarded as the most sophisticated, entailing as they do impersonal agents as the culprits. Since the mystical theories are less concerned with social forces than the other explanations, they are at first glance less interesting to the social anthropologist and have consequently received much less attention and also comparatively rare. As Mary Douglas (1966) has demonstrated, basic human processes of cognition may inform these theories.

More widespread, however, are the theories of animistic causation, which imply the existence of personalized, supernatural entities. In accordance with this kind of explanation, disease may be caused by the occasional departure of a person's own soul, as in the case of soul loss, but much more frequently through spirit aggression.

Theories of magical causation are found in a large number of different cultures and are manifest in two main forms: witchcraft and sorcery. In witchcraft-beliefs it is assumed that some human beings possess an evil force that may cause disease and misfortune. The force is supposed to be activated mainly by negative emotions, such as envy and hatred. There is no measure of technology and knowledge involved. The evil force is activated automatically, sometimes even without the conscious knowledge of the witch, as demonstrated by E. E. Evans-Prichard in his classical monograph *Witchcraft, Oracles and Magic among the Azande* (1937). Sorcery, on the other hand, is based on knowledge and technology. A sorcerer has knowledge of medicines and spells, and may apply these to a doll representing the person he or she wants to hurt, or to a piece of the victim's clothing, hair, or nail-clippings (just to mention one common procedure among sorcerers). Witch-craft and sorcery are often combined and, one is tempted to say, confused with one another. In strict anthropological terms, the witches of popular belief in Europe were really sorcerers, who sometimes acquired their evil powers from the Devil himself. It is commonly assumed that the demise of these theories in modern societies is due to superior knowledge of the laws of nature. Several observations indicate, however, that knowledge of the laws of nature in itself is not sufficient to explain why supra-natural theories are of marginal and mainly psychiatric interest in the modern world.

The demise of these theories took place over time, possibly as an integral part of the great transformation of society that started in the sixteenth century, and which has run its full course in our time. It can thus be seen as part of the breakthrough of the particular form of reason that is an integral part of modern Western thinking, and relates not only to the understanding of nature, but also to the understanding of the modes of organization of both government and economics.

That it is not merely the result of pure cognition, divorced from the context of social life, has been demonstrated by Trevor-Roper (1970), who points out that belief in witchcraft and sorcery in the sixteenth and seventeenth centuries, the age of reason, was not a "lingering ancient superstition, only waiting to dissolve. It was a new explosive force, constantly and fearfully expanding with the passage of time. . . . It was forewarned by the cultivated popes of the Renaissance, by the great Protestant reformers, by the saints of the Counter-Reformation, by the scholars, lawyers, and churchmen of the age of Scaliger and Lipsius, Bacon and Grotius, Béralle and Pascal" (cited in Marwick 1970, p. 121).

The demise of these beliefs after the great European witch-craze falls together with the gradual transformation of the *medieval village*. The general breakthrough of the scientific world view in general and theories of illness and misfortune in particular therefore probably owe as much to the development of a market economy and bureaucratic management as to knowledge itself.

The fact that many, even when exposed to the ideas of modern medicine, do not resign their beliefs in witchcraft and sorcery clearly demonstrates that knowledge that does not articulate with the experience of everyday life remains hidden (Brøg-ger 1971). The final triumph of the rational world view that relegates supernatural theories to the despised realm of superstition was therefore secured in large measure by the modern arts of administration and accounting.

In order to fully appreciate why these dimensions of human organization cleared the way for the scientific world view, we must reach beyond the formal properties of these dimensions to the concrete social context. As demonstrated in a recent work (Brøgger 1986), theories of illness and misfortune clearly relate to the ways in which individuals and their relationships to the community are articulated.

The most important dimension of this relationship is the structure of dependency: the organization of the relationships through which an individual ac-quires the indispensable necessities of life, material and immaterial. As long as these relationships remain personal, in the sense that the crucial individuals and groups are within the realm of a potential face-to-face order, they translate into ideas of witchcraft, sorcery, and spirit aggression. Relationships of this nature are characteristic of the *medieval village*.

To understand the psychology behind this translation does not require any measure of complex analysis. As long as a human being is crucially dependent upon a comparatively small number of known individuals, their power may easily be overestimated. Because they are firmly in control of the social destiny, the belief that they also may influence the unknown and hidden forces of nature does not seem farfetched.

Through the rise of *urban society* made possible by the introduction of bureau-cracy, formal jurisprudence, money and markets, these crucial relationships have been depersonalized. Thus they are given a measure of predictable rationality that reduces the visible influence of individual fellow human beings and makes it possible for the individual to rise above a sensitive concern for the capricious unreliability of human sentiments. Thus not only nature but also human society is relieved of its mystique and brought under the laws of rationality. This seems to be the social condition for the breakthrough of the modern, scientific world view.

In the local communities where this great transformation has not yet run its full course, supra-natural theories of disease and misfortune still linger on. A closer examination of the most essential human relationships in Nazaré will demonstrate to what degree they have retained their communal character, and consequently will also serve as a test of our assumption with regard to the social origin of supra-natural theories.

Three areas will be examined. The social network through which individuals derives their basic identity and emotional support, and the organization of housing will be examined in this chapter. The organization of fishing will be discussed in the next chapter.

THE MATRILINEAGE IN NAZARÉ

As we have already seen, the system of kinship and marriage in Nazaré favors the emergence of matrilineally extended families. Even in cases where full-fledged extended families do not emerge, individuals are identified with a matrilineage. Although these lineages rarely extend beyond three generations, they are essential for the organization of kinship relationships.

These lineages emerge with visible contours in the case of conflicts. When Maria Cândida, whom we have already referred to in the first chapter, has a disagreement with someone, she will demand strict loyalty from all her dependents. She will declare that from today relationships with such and such person must be terminated. This may sometimes be most inconvenient for the in-married man, if the declaration of persona non grata is crossed by previous ties of family or friendship.

The solution to a problem of this order will usually be solved through avoidance and/or delivery of secret messages to the person in question. If not, diplomatic relationships will be broken for an indefinite period of time. The whole lineage may also be involved if the lesser members are filing legitimate complaints against a person.

A lineage will frequently be known by the nickname of its most senior female members. The lineage of *Didala* may serve as a typical example.

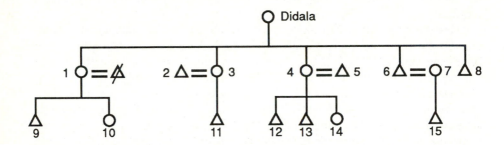

All the descendants of *Didala* are known as *Didalas*. The nickname of in-marrying males will usually yield to that of the lineage with regard to the offspring. The males themselves will, however, retain their own nicknames. But they may in a corporate context be referred to as *Didalas*. In this particular case 2 and 5 both had well established family nicknames. Their children may in certain contexts be referred to by the nicknames of their fathers. Thus 11 would, when he alone is concerned, be referred to as *Cinquenta*, likewise 12, 13, and 14 will be referred to as *Varredores,* in accordance with their father's nickname. When the whole lineage is concerned, however, they will be classified as *Didalas*.

In a particular case when a person falls out with 13, he immediately becomes persona non grata for the whole lineage, a destiny that also befalls members of his own lineage. As long as the conflict is unresolved, they will treat each other as non-persons and refuse to talk to each other. A consistent pattern of matrilineal nicknaming, however, does not emerge. There are too many exceptions for this pattern to be claimed as the general rule. The crucial factor seems to be the prominence of the nickname. A man with a particularly strong nickname earned by his lineage of origin may transmit this to his offspring. Yet there are situations in which he and his offspring will be classified with his wife's lineage.

On certain occasions the lineage will emerge as a visible corporation as for example during the communal festivals, such as the celebrations of *A Nossa Senhora da Vitória,* the patron Virgin of fishing, of St. John, and other important patron saints. During one particular St. John's celebration when pyres are lit in the streets, one of the streets of Nazaré was dominated by two lineages under the formidable leadership of two women. Because of a forthcoming marriage, the two families were joined in the celebration of St. John. They congregated outside the house of one of the matriarchs, one of the lineages thus appearing more or less as guests. It was the home territory of *Didala*. Because Joaquim, number 8 in the chart above, was going to marry Clara, the daughter of Judite, Judite was present with some of her married daughters and one unmarried son. One of the in-married husbands as well as her own husband were absent on this occasion.

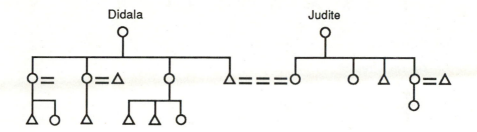

The occasion did not call for any particular ritual, and common celebrations of this sort are not institutionalized. Judite's visit was probably a show of good will because the marriage was to be celebrated in a nice way, *um casamento bonito,* and not forced through an elopement.

The members of the lineage share an interest in the estate of the matriarch, in this particular case a valuable house. Without a common interest of this sort, the lineage does not appear to have the same strength. But a measure of cooperation is to be expected. Members of the same lineage are expected to help each other through the extension of credit and consolation in distress, and serve as the first links in a network through which various benefits can be solicited: job opportunities, house rentals, support in conflicts, and a number of unpredictable tokens of assistance that may be necessary.

The prestige of an individual is to a certain degree determined by the standing of the lineage. A Nazareno normally cannot afford to break completely with his lineage, neither the lineage of his birth nor the lineage of his wife. Unless he is extremely successful and thus can afford more independence, his lineage is his only stable and comparatively predictable source of support.

Obviously this gives the women a more secure position than the men, who normally will be adopted by the lineage of their wives. For the men, however, the lineage of their mothers serves as an alternative source of support if the lineage of a man's wife for some reason fails to assist him, or in case of divorce. But as long as he has sisters, he will be regarded as a second class member of the lineage. Even unmarried sons who are still living at home will rank below their brothers-in-law. This will sometimes create an unbearable tension and cannot be sustained for long by a man of some initiative.

Even in a case where a wife moved to her husband's house, she gradually gained complete control in spite of the fact that a brother of her husband was living next door. Her dominance was dramatically emphasized on the occasion of the birthday party of her youngest son Paulo.

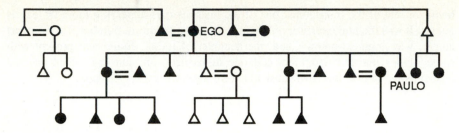

● ▲ Present

○ △ Non Present

None of her husband's family was invited, not even the brother next door. Her own brothers were invited, however, testifying to a somewhat unusual relationship between sister and brothers. Her eldest son and his children were absent.

Another son, recently married, however, was present with his wife and child. He was in a tug of war with his wife, who disapproved of this relationship to his brother Paulo. He gave the following description of the situation:

> Since I married, my relationship with my younger brother Paulo has been a source of conflict with my wife. The arguments she presents against him are of various kinds. Sometimes she will accuse me of wanting to behave like a bachelor, running after beautiful girls with my brother; on other occasions she will accuse Paulo of not showing any generosity towards her son. He only gives presents to others (the children of my sister who live near my mother).
>
>   Paulo often comes to visit me. Now and then he tells me that he is afraid of being badly received by my wife. Actually it has already happened. He has already learned to interpret some signs of her mood. If she doesn't give him a cup of coffee or a cake that she gives to other people, he understands that it's time to move out.

In spite of the closeness to his brother, Pedro is gradually being alienated from the lineage of his mother. This is not merely because of the manipulations of his wife's lineage. It is obvious that his mother no longer counts on him as a full-fledged member of her group.

When she received an unexpected windfall because an unmarried son, critically wounded in the war in Angola, was granted a pension and received 400.000$ in back payment, she did not disclose the full amount to her married sons. (The Portuguese use the dollar sign to represent their currency, the *escudo*, placing the sign between the escudo and its fraction of 100, the *centaro*. Thus, 10$5 indicates 10 escudos and 5 centaros; 400.000$ is equivalent to about $2800.00 in United States of America dollars.) She told them she had merely received 100.000$, and granted them only a few thousand each. In spite of her comparatively comfortable economy, she is very reluctant to help her married sons. Both of them are therefore dependent on the generosity of their adopted lineage in case of need.

Because of the unpredictable fortunes in fishing, the majority are from time to time forced to rely on loans from their more fortunate lineage mates. This is particularly the case during the winter months when fishing becomes impossible because of bad weather. Before fishing picks up in the spring months, credit becomes essential in order to get the basic necessities for the family. Credit is generally granted by the merchants, but when this source is exhausted, they have to rely on the loans extended by the more prosperous lineage members.

The lineage provides each individual with a set of non-negotiable relationships of great importance. Although some of the relationships may be temporarily inactive, and intense conflicts may sometimes develop within a lineage, it does provide its members with their basic identities as Nazarenos. The social standing of each individual is to some degree dependent upon the standing of the lineage to which he or she belongs. Although a man is to a large degree adopted by the lineage of his wife, he will always in certain contexts be identified by his lineage of origin, and he will eventually claim his share in the inheritance when his parents die. Through marriage and consanguinal ties, openings to a number of other lineages are available to most Nazarenos. Although most of these ties are inactive at any one time, they serve as a reserve of potential social credit that provides the villagers with that particular sense of belonging no longer existing in a cosmopolitan, urban setting. These emotional ties to the lineage are crucial to the well-being of the individual, and an individual who falls out with his lineage will normally experience great psychological strains.

The force of the lineage was demonstrated with particular drama one morning during the winter when the Nazarenos became aware of the black robes below the precipice of Sitio about 100 meters above the northern end of Nazaré. As this is the dreaded spot of ritual suicide, everyone immediately understood that they were witnesses to the last part of an emotional drama of tragic proportions. The wretched body of an old woman was carried down on a stretcher by her sons, who were visibly shaken. The drama had been provoked by the death of the mother of the victim. Because she had five sons and only one daughter, her control of the lineage was rather shaky. Her only daughter had left Nazaré to run a restaurant in a rural village nearby and was comparatively independent of her mother. A few months before the suicide, she had fallen out with her daughter. When her sons at the death of her mother wanted their share of the inheritance, she faced the prospect of losing her house. The death of her mother in fact provoked the fragmentation of her lineage because she had not succeeded in carrying it on through her daughter. Her sons were all married, and their residual loyalty to the mother's lineage was not sufficient to prevent its dissolution. Without the support of the lineage, her very existence was threatened, and suicide appeared to her as the only alternative left to her. That at least would serve as a dramatic punishment of her sons.

This, incidentally, explains why mothers usually prefer daughters rather than sons, and sometimes are visibly upset at the birth of boys. A Nazareno's standing is to a large extent determined by the standing of his lineage of origin. If he is from a poor lineage of low status, it would require great personal success to avoid the stigma of origin. The existence of an unofficial hierarchy of lineages is at odds with the egalitarian values to which the Nazarenos subscribe. This is but another aspect of the conflict between excellence and equality which, because of the unpredictable fortunes of fishing, is particularly pronounced in Nazaré. This hierarchy is primarily based on merit, above all economic merit. The possession of a house, the quality of the furniture and the interior decoration of the apartment, the possession of boats and equipment, and the performance at sea or in the marketing of fish are all essential for the prestige of a lineage. The meritocratic nature of the hierarchy, the system of inheritance, and the lack of parental control of marriages conspire to prevent any measure of stratification, and make the hierarchy most unstable and usually restricted to the lifespan of the leading matriarch.

A PARIAH GROUP IN THE FOLK COMMUNITY

At odds with the shifting nature of success and social standing is the existence of a pariah group of two lineages, which for several generations have sustained a marginal existence in Nazaré.

The most notorious of these lineages bears the nickname *Requeira,* which also serves as a derogatory term in the local dialect. The other is the *Corvos,* which is the process of disappearing and suggests that the status of the pariahs is of a temporary nature. The *Requeira,* however, were during the time of fieldwork at the peak of their notorious career. Particularly, the children of the *Requeira* are living up to the reputation of their lineage. Despised and feared by other children, they usually keep to themselves in the southern part of Nazaré. If they visit the center of Nazaré, they will always come together, easily visible in their dirty rags, combining begging with petty mischief.

The Nazarenos regard the *Requeira* as a separate caste. Few of them are fishermen, and they are suspected of subsisting as criminals. The fact that two of the men of the lineage were in jail during fieldwork suggests that the suspicions are not unfounded. Some of the women are believed to be prostitutes. This may not be true, but their family life is certainly disorderly, and they obviously have problems getting marriage partners among the other Nazarenos. Because of the reluctance of Nazarenos to marry members of the *Requeira's* lineage, they present a deviant pattern of household composition. The *Requeira* men remain in the household, and their habitat appears more or less like a disorderly camp to which brothers and sisters bring partners they have succeeded in recruiting either from outside rural communities, or from underprivileged and marginal Nazarenos.

There is a measure of promiscuity and also of endogamy in the camp. One of the in-marrying males had children both with a mother and her daughter. An unusual constellation of kinship-relations thus emerges: one man became, as it were, his own father-in-law. This mercurial partner was at the time of fieldwork in jail and was later killed in a fight. Some members of the *Requeira's* lineage are scattered around in the underprivileged margins of the village. The majority, however, live as squatters in the southern outskirts of Nazaré, where they live fairly close to each other in miserable, self-made shacks of wood, forming a rag-tag camp community.

The matriarch of the south-end *Requeira* is Maria *Requeira,* 77 years old. A close examination of her descendants reveals that of her five sons, all but one live in the camp. Her fourth son lives as squatter in a different part of Nazaré. One of her two daughters is married to a local fisherman and is integrated into the community.

Her eldest daughter lives in the camp and appears to be able to continue as the lineage matriarch at the eventual death of her mother.

Five of the second generation *Requeira,* starting with Maria, live in the camp. Of the third generation, three are married and also live in the camp, one man and two women. Together, they had at the time of fieldwork 22 minor children, forming a most unusual bilaterally extended family.

Of the seven mature men in the second and third generation, six have remained in the camp. Five of them are married. Three of them have married women from outside of Nazaré. The two others have married sisters of men who have married into the lineage. One has married the sister of his stepfather; the other his sister-in-law.

Of the four married women of the second and third generation, one, as mentioned, has married into the community; of the three who have remained, one has married a cousin and the two others marginal losers, one of them a notorious criminal. It is notable that all the married women, except the youngest who has not been married more than a couple of months, have had more than one husband.

The composition of the lineage of Maria *Requeira* is presented in tabular form below. The same data, in a more visual form, can be seen in the accompanying kinship chart.

The marriage pattern of the *Requeira* lineage explains its almost caste-like isolation. The marriages fail to scatter male members among the established lineages, and the in-marrying wives either are marginal or from outside communities. This pattern is followed by the Requeira sisters, and therefore the lineage remains without the infrastructure of kinship options characteristic of the Nazaré.

To be marginal is really to be without a respectable lineage. In the pre-bureaucratic community of Nazaré, an independent civic status outside the framework of kinship is not feasible. The marginalization of the *Requeiras* is the obvious result of a failure to establish adequate ties with the community through marriages. This demonstrates how the sins of the fathers in a prebureaucratic community are paid for by later generations. This process of marginalization is probably not unique, but rather representative of the establishment of pariah groups in kinship-dominated communities of the village type.

Although the average Nazareno is not without compassion, he does not regard the miserable condition of the *Requeira* children as victims of destiny who deserve understanding, support, and care. The idea that the community itself is responsible for the marginalization of the *Requeira* is completely alien to his mentality.

This reminds us of the fact that the modern welfare attitude towards marginal groups is a comparatively recent phenomenon. It germinated with the rise of the bourgeois culture and has reached its most articulate form in the modern bureaucratic state. If the case of the *Requeiras* is at all representative of the situation of marginal groups in prebureaucratic Europe, it suggests that ostracism is the characteristic reaction to deviance beyond a certain limit. This is so because members of a community, sustained by comprehensive, face-to-face relationships cannot risk the odium of contamination that a normal relationship to marginal persons implies. During fieldwork I sometimes got explicit warnings not to get involved with marginal persons, because my reputation would suffer. I was com-

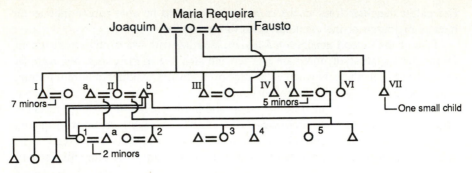

Maria Requeira
a) Joaquim Faustino
b) Fausto
Children: I João Requeira
        II Cândida
        III Jaime
        IV Joaquim
        V Victor
        VI Isabel
        VII Fausto

I	João Requeira, married Maria de Asunção, from rural village
	7 minor children
II	Cândida married, living in the camp
	a) João
	b) António
	4 grown-up children with first husband
	2 minor children with second husband
	1. Florinda, married, living in the camp
	a) César
	b) António, her mother's former lover
	2 minor children with first husband
	3 minor children with second husband
	2. Saul, married to a woman from Peniche, living near the camp
	3. Laura, married to a distant cousin, living in the camp
	4. Bruno, unmarried, in jail
	5. 2 minor children
III	Jaime, married to sister of mother's second husband, living in the camp
IV	Joaquim, living as a squatter in a different part of Nazaré
V	Victor, married to the sister of Cândida's second husband, living in the camp, but has later illegally occupied a vacant house nearby
	5 minor children
VI	Isabel, married to a fisherman, and is integrated into the community
VII	Fausto, married to a French woman, now separated, living with a small child in the camp

pelled to heed these warnings, feeling at the time the chilling threat of communal sanctions.

    Only when relationships with marginal people can be sustained through specialized and protected channels is a measure of integration feasible. Relationships of this order cannot be sustained by a folk community because it lacks the refined concept of role-specialization through which roles may be kept apart and consummated separately.

    The process of ostracism that is the logical outcome of the dynamics of social relationships in the *village-type community* then seems to be responsible for the formation of the subculture of criminals and vagrants who infested prebureaucratic

Europe, creating the homebred pariahs that in certain areas were hardly distinguish-able from alien pariahs like the gypsies (Sundt 1850). It is fair to assume that the caste-like nature of these pariah-groups emerged above all from their lack of ability to contract affinal relationships outside their own groups and the consequent formation of endogamous units at the margin of society.

ASCRIBED RELATIONSHIPS AS THE CONTRACTUAL MODEL

Although the shallow lineages in Nazaré cannot compete in importance with lineages in most tribal societies, they provide each individual with a firm structure of ascribed relationships. Through marriages, equally firm relationships are es-tablished. Although based on a contract, a marriage is neither limited in time nor in content. The destiny of every grown-up Nazareno is thus in a large degree de-termined by a limited group of people with whom relationships are face-to-face and comprehensive.

As we have already seen, when a new family is established, housing is in principle the responsibility of the mother-in-law. But few new families are in fact able to procure this basic necessity. The Nazarenos explain that formerly most families owned their houses, but that during the crisis in the thirties, the price of fish declined dramatically and many families had to live on credit. The main source of credit for the daily bread was in fact the local baker, who would insist that his clients put up their houses as collateral when they failed to pay their bills within a reasonable period of time. In this way the baker became the largest real-estate owner in Nazaré. Although this process probably explains how a number of families lost the ownership of their houses, a number of other families would have been compelled to rely on the capitalist real-estate market even if their parents had not belonged to the unfortunates who lost their houses to the baker. The average home of a fisherman would rarely be sufficient to accommodate all their children, making all but one or two dependent on the market.

When the basic necessity for accommodation has to be procured through an impersonal, capitalist market, it could be expected that the fishermen would be attuned to the impersonal rationality of the contract-dominated urban society, and thus be less prone to the traditional superstitions of the medieval village. This, however, does not seem to be the case, a supposition confirmed not only by the common beliefs held by the Nazarenos, as we shall see, but also by a number of mystic experiences reported by house tenants.

HAUNTED HOUSES AND DEPENDENCY

A couple in their forties tell the following story: "When we were newly married, we were living in a house with two floors. Because we did not feel comfortable on the ground floor, we moved to the first. One night we heard a cracking sound down-stairs. We went down to see what had happened, and noticed that a jar which had been in the middle of the table was gone. We were afraid to remain in the house and went to sleep in the house of my [the wife's] mother. Next morning when we came back to the house, the jar was on the floor broken in a thousand pieces."

The mother went to a witch (bruxa) who told them that cause of the incident was the spirit of the first owner of the house. The spirit wanted them to arrange for a requiem mass for him so that he could go to heaven.

Rosa, a woman of fifty, tells the following story: "Fifteen years ago my husband was possessed by the devil. He was also possessed by the spirit of two men who had hanged themselves. My husband sometimes had conversations with the wall. He stopped working." One night in her sleep she felt a heavy burden weighing her down. She wanted to scream, but was unable to. She fought with the burden until she woke up and was able to scream. Then she understood that her husband was really suffering. She tried to lift his arm. When he finally woke up, she told him: "Let us get away from this house." They left the house for four months.

She went to a witch. During the session with the bruxa, a spirit appeared, threatened her, and said he would hurt her if he got a chance. (The woman explained that she possessed a particular force that made her immune to the attacks of the spirit.) She had a tough quarrel with the spirit who revealed himself as the former owner of the house. She then told the spirit that she would burn him out: Háss de ficar todo queimado. (This refers to the ritual of cleaning the house with smoke.)

Another spirit who possessed her husband also appeared during the session. He had killed himself in the house next to the one she rented. Her neighbor, who was renting this house, had told her that she had seen a coffin on the bed.

The bruxa told her that the spirits had entered the head of her husband through a small opening in his temple, that he was now freed from these spirits, but that the devil was still in him. However, her husband would now be able to work. The bruxa warned her that she should be particularly careful when her husband went to the cabana, the shed on the beach, because the devil could strangle him with the ropes that were stored there, i.e., entice him to commit suicide.

The particular house they rented was out of line with the others, protruding a few centimeters out in the street, a fact that made it vulnerable to the attack of the spirits. Later the woman had established herself with her own house and had been free from supernatural interference until she started losing weight and feeling extremely weak spiritually. When she had lost 20 kilograms she again consulted a bruxa. During the session the bruxa told the woman she had a problem with her daughter. The woman replied that she was on good terms with all of her daughters. The bruxa then explained that her daughter had a problem and it was this problem that made her nervous: "The problem concerns people who are not of your own blood. It is concerning a house, the owner of the house of your daughter is attacking you with black magic (feitiçaria, bruxaria). It was the owner of the house who made you sick. She attacked you in your moment of weakness. Normally you have a strong spiritual force (corrente). Your daughter must get away from this house, otherwise her life will not be happy (hão corre bem)."

Incidentally, the temporary weakness that was affecting this woman, which she described as corrente fraca, appeared when she had problems with the reconstruction of her house and her expenses soared beyond the estimate. Because her income and expenses were closely monitored as a part of an investigation of the household economy in the village, it was possible to observe the close coincidence of the onset of her spiritual frailty *(corrente fraca)* with the peak of her expenses.

The income and expenses both of herself and her daughter are plotted in the accompanying figure. Her troubles started in the month of March, when the gap between income and expenses soared for both mother and daughter. This coincidence suggests that her feelings of spiritual vulnerability are a translation of her economic worries into the idiom of spirit belief.

Whether the *bruxa* cynically framed the problems of the woman by linking them to a common Nazareno concern or she truly believed her explanation to be authentic and inspired is difficult to know. What is beyond doubt is that somewhat mysterious afflictions of the kind reported by this woman are often believed to be caused by the spirits of haunted houses, *casas assombradas*. The *bruxa* therefore could make a fairly safe guess, informed by her many years of experience with afflicted Nazarenos.

It is commonly believed that there are many empty houses in Nazaré because people are afraid to live in them because of the spirits. However, to have these houses pointed out was not possible. The significant fact therefore is the belief. It confirms the fact that among the Nazarenos houses are not regarded only as a commodity, subject to rational, commercial transactions. A mystical communion is believed to exist between a house and its original owner, or sometimes with previous inhabitants.

Although houses in many cases are procured through a capitalist real-estate market, the fishermen do not fully appreciate the non-personal nature of a contract. Rather than being attuned to the impersonal nature of unistranded relationships, the fishermen bring the ethos of the village beyond its sphere of relevance, and symbolically transform the contract relationship into a personal and emotionally charged social reality. This is in tune with their experiences in everyday life, where transactions with their fellows never are devoid of personal significance. Economic transactions completely divorced from human relationships are foreign to the mentality of the Nazarenos.

It is probably true, as Reddy (1984) argues, that the commercial attitude of capitalist exchange developed gradually and, contrary to common belief, was not part of the general consciousness even in the nineteenth century, the heroic age of liberal economics. Only after protracted exposure to the capitalist mode of production and market exchange did a genuine market culture emerge. As Reddy has convincingly demonstrated, not even the great strikes in the late eighteenth century, when the workers and the owners of the French textile mills were pitted against each other in a bargain over remuneration and rules of work, can be taken as evidence of a genuine labor market. Neither the workers nor their patrons conceived of human labor as a commodity. To both parties their relationship was conceived as paternalistic, more feudal than commerical.

In a similar vein, the Nazarenos are not conscious of a perfect real-estate market in which the price of housing is the outcome of supply and demand independent of human emotions and considerations. Although a house contract does not imply a consummated human relationship, it is nevertheless invested with the sentiments of communality in which the unpredictable capriciousness of human emotions are

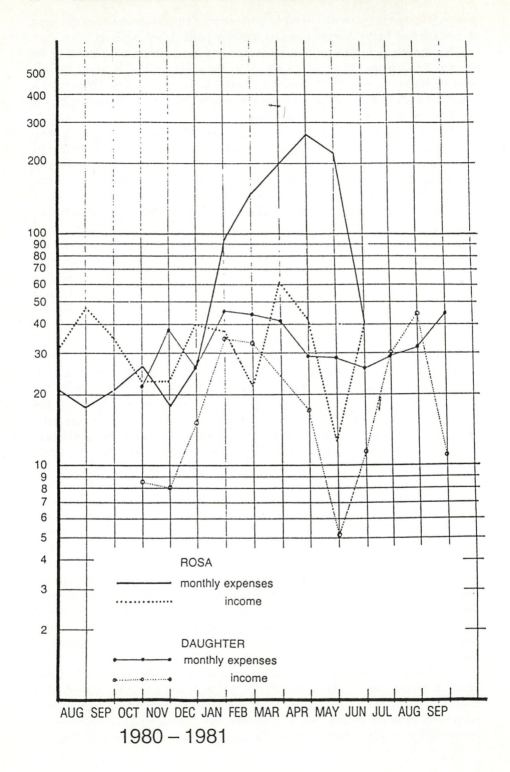

believed to operate. If the original owner of the house is absent, or even dead, he is believed to be acting as if he was party to a communal, unlimited relationship. Even if a tenant does not have any problems with the actual owner, misfortunes and afflictions are nevertheless often taken as proof of a disturbed relationship. Moreover, ownership of a house is no guarantee against supernatural interference, because the original owner or even a former tenant may still be attached to it. If later owners or heirs act in undesirable ways, the original owners may appear to show their concern.

Laurinda, who is renting the house of Venâncio, son of Fransisco, was disturbed by strange noises during the night, and neither she nor her family were able to sleep for a long time. Once during the night she could smell the fumes of tobacco and saw a man sitting on a chair in the dark. It was resolved that this was the spirit of Venâncio Peres, one of the former owners. The reason for his interference was that his nephew Venâncio wanted more than his legitimate part of the house, which had been the joint property of Venâncio Peres and his brother Fransisco before they passed away.

In most human societies the shelter of the family is the symbolic space par excellence. It is the locus of the hearth, which often is chosen as a symbol of communion, and closely associated with the common meal. As the domain of women it also becomes associated with fertility and the mystery of life, and as the place of rest for the old, frail and sick it also frames the emotionally charged moments of departure and death. It protects its inhabitants in their most vulnerable states in love and in sleep.

The strongest of human emotions become attached to the house. Even when it is empty it appears strangely alive, as if the memories of a complex of human lifecycles were symbolically condensed in its space. Few human beings, even those of a modern, materialistic attitude to life and death, are insensitive to the symbolic qualities of a house that has sheltered generations of human beings.

It is as object of symbolic space the houses provoke the imagination of the Nazarenos, and serve as a stage for the projection of a complex of feelings, hidden fears, ideas, and memories that bring to life the spirits of past owners and residents, as well as the strange resonance of sounds, which, framed by the suspicious mind, become charged with social meaning. Sensitivity to the symbolic quality of houses is part of traditional European culture and is not peculiar to the Nazarenos. What is peculiar is the frequency of experiences of this nature. In the modern, urbanized communities of Europe, stories of the haunted houses belong to the realm of tales and legends, and few people have any personal experience of this nature. In Nazaré, however, it is a living reality, and a number of completely sane and credible people have had personal encounters with spirits, have been haunted by strange and frightening sounds, and have even smelled the fumes of tobacco from visiting spirits.

It is commonly assumed that not only belief in witchcraft, but also belief in the spirits, was conquered by the superior knowledge of the laws of nature that emerged with the age of reason. As suggested, this explanation is too simple because it disregards the social factors in the development as well as in the acceptance of knowledge in general.

The disenchanted world that emerged with the breakthrough of positive science was not conceived in a social vacuum, and in order to fully understand its unique historic development, it must be studied against its existential background. It is no mere coincidence that the enchanted world of spirits and supernatural beliefs gave way to the modern world view with the disintegration of the medieval village. As the case of Nazaré demonstrates, the enchanted world still exists where human relationships have retained their communal nature. A considerable part of the population of Nazaré believes in the traditional supernatural world not out of ignorance, but because it is in tune with their experience of everyday life. In the age of TV, every man, woman and child in Nazaré has been thoroughly exposed to the modern world. But, as we shall see, it is only when the structure of their dependency with regard to the community changes that they are prepared to give up their ancient beliefs. Exposure to the capitalist real-estate market was not sufficient to impose a rational, commercial attitude to housing. Instead, the pattern of non-limited, personal relationships that dominates most spheres of their lives invades the contractual relationship. Seen at a close range, the contract did not basically change the nature of their dependency, although it took some of the edge off the relevance of unpredictable sentiments.

Every Nazareno is in the grip of his lineage, bound by relationships he cannot permanently dismiss in any meaningful way. Even if he impatiently dismisses a relationship, as is often the case, it is not ended, but simply becomes latent, a potential threat to his well-being. The festering wounds of disturbed relationships between people bound by indissoluble ascriptive ties provides the seedbed of witchcraft.

Although houses in the majority of cases are procured through the capitalist real-estate market, contractual relationships to owners are dominated by the ethos of communality and are perceived as human relationships, not judicially circumscribed and limited affairs. In spite of the contract and the trappings of bureaucracy and law, the Nazarenos perceive the relationship to the owner as a personal relationship, and conflicts easily provoke that paranoic state of mind that is institutionalized in beliefs in witchcraft and sorcery.

In order to protect themselves against the mystical assault of sorcery, Nazarenos not only wish their houses to be blessed by holy water, but also purified through the folk ritual of fuming. When threatened by disease or misfortune, they take care to ward off the effects of evil medicines and spirits by the fumes of the burning fronds of Easter palms charged with the power of holy water.

Supernatural problems associated with houses, however, are not only restricted to the influence of the owner. As we saw in the case of Rosa and her husband, the Devil and unknown spirits may appear together with the spirit of the deceased owner.

In the following story troubled family relations are manifested in a haunted house. It is being told by one of the main *curandeiras* of Nazaré, commonly referred to as *bruxa*:

> Husband and wife heard a lot of noise in their house. They heard footsteps and the movement of things. They were unable to sleep, and suffered terribly from insomnia and headaches. In the darkness of night the wife recognized a person she had known alive, her sister-in-law. She had been widowed and she went to live with her brother. Thus the

wife [who is consulting the *curandeira*] had to take care of her. She was evil and tried to trouble the relationship between husband and wife, and complained to her brother about her sister-in-law when he came home. Because the brother knew that his sister was evil, he did not pay much attention to her, but occasionally he had trouble with his wife because of her. She was a rich woman, and when she died, she left everything to her brother. But she caused much sorrow because she had disregarded her other relatives and was not received by God. Her body was in its grave, but her spirit remained in the house of her sister-in-law. Because of this, the woman heard strange noises and battering windows and even saw the spirit of her deceased sister-in-law. . . . Just yesterday she appeared again. The woman was having trouble with her husband and they hardly spoke to each other. Yesterday she asked, as she saw the spirit: "What do you want from me, Lurdes?" The spirit answered: "I want you to forgive me. I was treating you badly when I was alive on the earth" *(Eu fui muito má para ti na terra)*. As she did when she was alive *(a virar-lhe a cara, e a fazer-lhe carantonhas e mau olhado)*, she was causing trouble, quarrels and evil eye. Her husband may not drink, because he has a very weak mind *(cérebro muito fraco)*. And when he has been drinking, he is a danger both to himself and his wife. I have advised her not to let her husband go alone to the cafes. Things are now getting better. Both husband and wife are now feeling much better. But they still hear noises in the house. The spirit is suffering many restrictions because she wished her brother and sister-in-law bad when she was alive. She needs an abundance of light. Her sister-in-law has already lit candles in front of her saints. This spirit is not alone, but is followed by a multitude of other spirits who are also in need of light. Yesterday I finished the treatment and the woman has asked me to bless the house with holy water. I started today treating the house with smoke to drive away the spirits *(fazer os defumadores)*.

The supernatural afflictions connected with houses show that both witchcraft, sorcery and spirit aggression appear as satisfactory explanations to the Nazarenos. This recalls Lewis' (1971) suggestion that "it may sometimes be more illuminating to discard the culturally grounded expressions 'spirit-possession' and 'witchcraft' altogether and think in terms of oblique and direct mystical attack" (p. 302). We might also add that sorcery should be excluded.

It has been demonstrated (Brøgger 1986) that the nature of "oblique and direct mystical attack" clearly relates to the structure of dependency between an individual and the community. The crucial dimensions seem to be ascribed versus acquired relationships or statuses on the one hand and dyadic versus corporative relationships on the other. Ascribed relationships, of course, are those an individual acquires at birth and as a member of his or her community. Acquired relationships are, as the name implies, contracted relationships. The dominant mode of the traditional village is the ascribed relationship, that of the urban society the acquired form. Dyadic relationships are limited to one alter, corporate relationships to "corporations" such as a lineage, an age grade, or social institutions like bureaucracies. These dimensions and their relationship to beliefs can be represented in the following diagram:

	Dyadic	Corporate
Ascribed	Witchcraft	Spirit aggression
Contractual	Sorcery	Political demonology

In a society where the essential necessities of life are acquired through ascribed, *dyadic* relationships, *witchcraft beliefs* will tend to prevail. This does not exclude sorcery, which may be found as a residual category. When ascribed, *corporate* relationships dominate, beliefs in *spirit aggression* seem to prevail. In cases where corporate, acquired relationships dominate, as in the modern, bureaucratic state political demonology may develop as a part of the belief-system. As we have seen, the Nazarenos are firmly tied to a limited number of people through both ascribed and contractual ties, which have been assumed to promote witchcraft and sorcery beliefs respectively.

A distinction must be made, however, between the limited contract characteristic of relationships in bureaucratic societies and non-specific contracts of neighborhood and ritual kinship. Only through the former is the relationship articulated in a rational, judicial form that minimizes the unpredictable vibrations of human sentiments. Although house contracts clearly are of the first kind, they are not perceived as such by many Nazarenos.

In the next chapter we shall examine the structure of relationships that may be assumed to promote theories of spirit aggression, i.e., the dependency upon groups of personally known individuals.

5 / The Social Organization of Fishing and the Structure of Relationships

In the preceding chapter we explored the relationship between beliefs in supernatural afflictions and the structure of social relationships. We have seen that social reality in Nazaré is dominated by ascribed relationships organized around the matrilineage. The importance of these relationships overshadows contractual relationships to a degree that they also prevail in relationships of a modern, bureaucratic nature, as in the case of housing contracts.

In the traditional village, the many-stranded relationships foster a non-limited field of interaction, where instrumental and rational matters are not always kept apart from personal matters and emotions, or the unpredictable and sometimes irrational interference of sentiments. It is precisely structures of relationships of this type that sustain such supernatural ideas of causation as witchcraft, sorcery, and spirit aggression.

In this chapter we will explore the structure of relationships determined by the organization of fishing. After a discussion of crucial differences between fishermen and peasants with regard to the main factors of production, fishing grounds, and land respectively, a description of fishing techniques will be presented. These are crucial to the organization of fishing and the composition of crews. Finally, the structure of relationships between crew-members and between crew-members and masters will be explored in order to determine how they may influence supernatural beliefs.

The major difference between fishermen and peasants is that the former have more or less free access to their main niche, where peasants are restricted by the system of ownership. The situation of the fishermen is somewhat similar to that of pastoral people: if we disregard questions of national territorial waters and modern claims to national economic zones, the sea is open. No one may claim exclusive ownership to the fishing grounds in part or in toto.

Although a system of licensing may restrict access to the sea, no measure of stratification at the local level can normally be related to differences in access to fishing grounds. Even if the Portuguese government practices a system of licensing and control, this does not in actual fact restrict the fishermen's access to the sea. Although regulation is theoretically possible, the situation in Nazaré does not prevent any fisherman from practicing the fishing technology of his choice and within his means, with the exception of net-fishing from the shore, the so-called *arte xávega.*

The situation recalls Radcliffe-Brown's classical distinction between joint and separate management (1952). The exploitation of fishing grounds rarely requires any measure of joint management. Just as a large tract of pasture may be exploited more or less independently by small groups of pastoralists, the exploitation of the fishing grounds does not require any measure of joint management between different enterprises.

This situation of course prevails only as long as the proportion of fishing units in relation to the extension of the fishing grounds remains below a certain critical point. As far as our present case is concerned, however, the fishing grounds can be regarded as free for all. This has obvious implications for the organization of fishing. At its present stage of development, different enterprises can act independently and do not require any measure of joint organization. This fact promotes an ethos of individualism strikingly different from the situation in most peasant societies. Whereas the peasants operate under the iron law of limited goods, the fishermen enjoy an unlimited access to the main niche.

The crucial factors, then, are the fisherman's access to equipment, on the one hand, his luck and that of his companions on the other. In order to grasp how these factors influence the relationship with his peers and the community, we shall examine the different technologies, locally called *artes,* and the composition and recruitment of crews.

THE ARTS OF FISHING

The fishing grounds off Nazaré stretch 80 kilometers parallel to the coast and stretch about 30 kilometers out into the Atlantic. Access to this parallelogram of fishing grounds is dependent upon the different types of boats available and various fishing techniques.

These fishing techniques may conveniently be classified in three main groups. The *arte xávega,* already mentioned, is restricted to the coastline, and is only practiced along the beach from the promontory to the north to the mouth of the Alcoa River to the south. The second group, which includes line and net-fishing, is mainly practiced in the bay area, but sometimes also on longer excursions. The third group corresponds to the larger vessels, the *botes do alto* and the *rapas,* which mainly exploit the high sea. Because our interest is focused on the social organization of the fishing, the discussion of the *artes* will not focus on all their technical detail, but only those features strictly relevant for social relations.

The *arte xávega* technique, as indicated, is practiced from the shore. A net is placed in a half circle in the sea and gradually pulled towards the shore by a land-based team. In order to spread the net, the so-called *barco de bico*—named for the peaked prow of the vessel that incidentally has become the emblem of Nazaré—is used. Because it has been built for the purpose of *arte xávega,* it has no keel. Its flat bottom is well adapted to the sands of the Nazareno beach. Since the importance of *arte xávega* has declined sharply in recent years, this specialized *barco de bico*

The arte xávega, *net-fishing from the shore, is more scenic than efficient. It promotes an atmosphere of excitement to the mixed crew of women, children, and older men.*

is no longer being built. Today the net is cast from a close relative of the *barco de bico,* the *candis,* a somewhat larger vessel with a less pronounced prow. The *candis*—so-called because when engaged in night-fishing it is provided with a lamp *(candela)* to attract the fish—is also used for net-fishing in the bay (described below).

Before the new port was taken into use, all the boats except the trawlers *(rapas)* were pulled ashore on the beach, traditionally with a pair of oxen, later with a tractor. In order to get the boats to sea, however, only manpower would do. It required dexterity and experience to launch the vessel through the surf. It was important to choose the right moment and avoid the larger waves, which could easily capsize the boat if not expertly maneuvered. Since the advent of the new port, only a few vessels remain on the beach, which some years back was thronged with the characteristically shaped boats of Nazaré. Painted in bright colors, each owner having his own pattern, they made a colorful and exotic spectacle, and are a favorite target of tourist snapshots. With their broad bottoms and beaks, they are crafts obviously well adapted to their unique sandy niche, providing the evolutionary tree of fishing vessels with an amphibious variety that now seems doomed to extinction. Only the few units of *arte xávega* keep the amphibious tradition alive. Although the brightly colored amphibians are still seen in the port, their particular shapes are no longer required, and will probably all be gone in a few years time.

The crew of *arte xávega* is the most heterogenous of the crews in Nazaré. Nowadays few grown men will engage themselves as crew in this *arte*. The crews consist primarily of women, old men, and children. Young and fit men are only required for the cast, and that does not require more than four men. The men will recruit a crew of from 12 to 20 women and a few children ages 7 to 14 to help pull the net ashore, an operation creating a movement of great excitement and a lot of joking. The *ésprit de corps* of the female crew is expressed in ribald jokes, horseplay, and teasing, which—at least with regard to sexual allusions—would rival any group of young men in a similar situation.

When the sack is ashore, the mood of the crew varies with the size of the catch. Great excitement is expressed at the sight of the gleaming fish. If the catch is next to nothing, frustration is expressed in rather crude terms, but not without that peculiar sense of humor that is characteristic of the Nazareno female. The sack is opened by one of the men and the crew proceeds to sort the valuable fish from the assortment of crabs, small octopuses, and other undesired specimens of shoreline fauna. The catch is divided between the participants, with the owner getting the lion's share. Today there are no more than ten boats in operation. The favored spots along the shore—known by names like *Borda do Poço* (the rim of the well), *Lanço Norte* (the Northern throw), *Lanço de Lama* (the mud throw)—are no longer thronged with the crews of *arte xávega*. At the peak of this type of fishing in 1924, 117 boats with crews competed for the favored spots.

The most picturesque of the fishing techniques is known as the *arte do candis*. As the name implies, this is a technique by which the fish are attracted by artificial light. Formerly, a formidable kerosene lamp was used; today a clear and penetrating light made by bottled gas is used. On quiet summer nights the lights from the *candis* on the fishing-grounds under the northern escarpment separating Nazaré from Sitio creates a marvellous effect. The small fleet of *candis,* framed by the elegantly curved beach in the foreground, the escarpment to the north, and the wide expanse of the sea to the west, is a sight of awe-inspiring beauty.

This ancient technique requires two boats, the *candis,* reminiscent of the *barco de bico,* but larger, and a smaller boat of a more streamlined and contemporary look, the *lancha*. The net used in *candis* fishing is rectangular, with meshes of 40–60 millimeters. The upper end is equipped with cork or plastic floats, the lower end a sinker of iron, and rings through which runs a rope the full length of the net. When the net is cast a strong-smelling bait consisting of the entrails of sardines, *carapau* (trachurus trachurus), and small fish is spread on the water, which together with the light serves to entice the fish into the net.

The net is dropped in a circle. Before the float above the iron sinker is reached, the *lancha* moves out, and the circle is closed. The men will then start pulling the rope so as to close "the purse" from the bottom. They then proceed to pull in the net. As the bottom of the net reaches the surface, the fishermen are frequently rewarded by the sight of a mass of writhing and gleaming fish. The crew normally consists of 7–9 men. The catch is divided by the number of fishermen involved plus three more parts. Each member of the crew receives one part. The owner of the boats and nets receives three parts, and another as a member of the crew.

Another time-honored technique is the so-called *chumbada* (*chumbo* = lead), a type of line-fishing. The line is provided with a lead sinker in the form of a pyramid. A short way beyond the sinker two shorter lines are attached to the main line, each with a hefty hook. Once the line has been cast, the fisherman ties the end of the line around his finger. At the slightest touch indicating the presence of a fish, he pulls instantly so as to hook the fish. This *arte* requires expert knowledge of the bottom of the sea and the depths because it is particularly aimed at the species hiding around rocks at the bottom, particularly the *safio* (clupea conger). *Chumbada*-fishing today is practiced from the smallest of the contemporary vessels, the *lancha* (consult the drawing on page 88). Usually two men will work together, each one keeping his own catch.

The outboard motor has increased the use of the *lancha,* which formerly was used primarily to assist the throwing of the net, as in the *arte dos candis.* Today it is not only used for *chumbada*-fishing, but also for the kind of net-fishing where the net is placed vertically like a straight wall in the sea, in which case it is referred to as *rede de emalhar.*

The size of the net holes are chosen according to the desired prey. For *pescada* (merluccius merluccius) and *faneca* (gadus luscus), the meshes should be 70 millimeters, for shellfish 80 millimeters. The nets may be of different sizes, usually 30 × 3.5 fanthoms *(braços).* The net is provided with floats and lead sinkers. The crew consists normally of two or three men. When fish are caught, the catch is divided in equal parts according to the number of men, an extra half part being given to the owner of the boat. In the case of shellfish, the owner receives half of the catch, and the other half is divided equally between the crew, including the owner, who thus receives more than half of the catch. This type of fishing is also practiced from somewhat larger motorboats, *botes do alto.* These boats normally have a crew of eight men. The catch is first divided in two. One part goes to the owner. The other part is divided in the following way: 1½ parts for the machinist, 3 parts for the menders of the net and 1 for each of the crew members. Usually the *botes do alto* will leave the nets in the sea for one or more days. To do so, both ropes of the net are provided with sinkers and floats.

The *traineiras* are seagoing vessels and can comfortably accommodate a crew of 20 men. The fishing net is set out from the *traineira,* but in order to harvest the catch two smaller boats of the *lancha* type are required. The main species of fish harvested with this equipment are *xaputa* (brama raii) and sword-fish.

A fishing technique that was practically dying out during fieldwork in the 1970s was the so-called *espinel* technique using long lines with hooks. In 1978–79 only ten were in operation, and two years later only one unit was active. The obvious reason for this was the decrease in the owners' share in the catch from 13 to 8 parts, which was the result of a strike. This gain made by the crews was merely temporary, however, because most of the units changed to net-fishing requiring a smaller crew. A number of fishermen therefore lost their position as crew members. This created considerable resentment, but no real unemployment, mainly because most of the surplus men were able to take up *lancha*-fishing, which required but a modest investment of 100.000$ in 1978.

The *espinel*-units, one after the other, changed to ringnet-fishing, at the present time the most important technique in Nazaré. The ringnet-boats are referred to as *cercadoras* or *rapas,* and are of the same kind as the *traineira.* The technique is similar to that of the *candis,* minus the light, the bait, and the *lancha.* Equipped with

TYPES	COMPARABLE MEASURES IN METRES
LANCHA	0.57 3.43 1.47
CANDIS	0.73 4.51 2.19
BOTE	0.92 7.87 2.56
BOTE TRAINEIRA	1.62 15.98 4.58

echo-sounder, the *rapas* are able to locate the fish shoals. This requires great skill on the part of the master, who is cruising the sea mainly according to his knowledge of the behavior of the shoals and his intuition. When he spots a shoal on the echo-sounder, he instructs the crew to drop the net while he himself navigates the boat in a circle to trap the shoal. The favored species are *carapau* and sardines.

The size of the crew is from 12 to 14 men, and the catch is divided in the following way: 10 parts for the owner; 8 parts for the equipment; 2 parts for the skipper, *mestre*, generally the owner; 1½ for the *contra-mestre*, subchief; 1½ for the machinist *(motorista);* 1¼ for the assistant machinist; and 1¼ for the whip *(chamador)*, who is responsible for summoning the crew when the skipper decides to go to sea. The other crew-members receive one part each. In addition, the unit sometimes keeps an old man ashore, who helps mending the net and keeping the equipment in order. Referred to as *velho de terra* (old man ashore), he receives ½ part.

ATTITUDE TO FORMAL ORGANIZATION

Romantic observers of the fishermen in Nazaré could easily be led to believe that they were watching ardent traditionalists who stick to their time-honored crafts. But the fact is that the fishermen eagerly exploit all the new possibilities offered by technological changes and economic opportunities. It is also true, however, that maximization of the catch is not the only consideration given to the choice of equipment and mode of organization.

A good case could probably be made for a larger measure of cooperation, both with regard to acquisition of expensive equipment and sharing of the spoils. If all the catches of the Nazarenos were pooled and evenly distributed, all of them could get comparatively comfortable and secure lives. Yet the Nazarenos seem to prefer a system that keeps some of them in abject poverty and makes a few of them wealthy beyond the wildest dreams of the average fisherman. Even when the government encouraged the establishment of cooperatives after the restoration of democracy on 25 April 1974, the Nazarenos were not willing to give it a try. When the matter was discussed, they would invariably point out the miserable destiny of the cooperatives organized in the neighboring fishing community of Peniche.

The lack of desire for cooperative venture among the fishermen of Nazaré has driven the few communist organizers who have given it a try into desperation. Active communists in Nazaré are not found among the fishermen. One communist leader was employed by the fishermen's health insurance organization, *Caixa Mútua dos Pescadores*. During a conversation with him in 1980, he became quite nostalgic about the revolution in 1974, when the communists for a period of time were dominating. Then the communists succeeded for the first and the only time to organize a strike in Nazaré. The main issue of the strike was to reduce the parts, *quinhões*, of the owners. The strike lasted for 40 days, and created a temporary standoff between the fishermen on one side and the owners on the other. The owners eventually gave in to the demands, but the situation of the fishermen did not really improve because the owners then rapidly changed from line-fishing to net-fishing and thus were able to reduce their crew considerably.

The strike had no lasting effect on the pattern of organization of the fishermen. The communist leader complained that the fishermen did not cooperate, that they lacked *espírito do unidade*. The trade union of fishermen in Nazaré came to a standstill because of a lack of funds. His explanation of this failure was that the fishermen had no political training, that they were unwilling to take responsibilities. If a meeting was called, no one appeared. They were too shy to speak to the representatives of the trade unions (only in the *tabernas* are they willing to speak). He complained that Nazaré was different from the rest of Portugal: "Laws passed in Lisbon are not respected in Nazaré, and a situation of apartheid exists between the bourgeoisie and the class of fishermen. They respect *Senhor Doutor* and are living in the spirit of fascism." Obviously his frustration was complete and he had lost all hope of organizing the fishermen politically.

What this young communist organizer had failed to appreciate was the power of the lineages and networks of kith and kin, as well as the fact that the situation of the fishermen is very different from that of industrial workers. The familial ties and the communal nature of their social relations are at odds with an organization of separate interests that fail to appreciate the many-stranded nature of the social structure. By joining a trade union, many fishermen would offend the obligations owed to the lineages. To be seen speaking to a *Kader* from the trade union is considered embarrassing. Only when safely surrounded by their fellows at the *tabernas* are they relieved of the onus of subverting their communal obligations by talking to a professional organizer.

For obvious reasons the fishermen of Nazaré do not share the mentality of industrial workers. That would go against the basic premise of their existence as fishermen. The cherished activity of the fishermen is what they refer to as *pesca á sorte*. This expression reveals one of the most important existential features of fishing, that of luck. The system of *quinhões* or *partes* gives each man a stake in the immediate proceeds of the enterprise. He is not a salaried worker. His situation is more similar to that of a hunter who stakes his fortune in the chase of an elusive and invisible prey. It is this fact that gives the pursuit of fishing its particular psychological appeal, which is revealed in many fishermen's consuming preoccupation with the forces of nature: the condition of the weather, the size of the waves constantly breaking on the sand of the beach, the temperature, and the directions and strength of the wind. All these signs have a bearing on the prospect of fishing and therefore are signs of the most profound importance. To the fully committed fisherman the humdrum variations of the weather take on an almost personal meaning, as if something akin to a conscious will lay behind and ruled it.

THE ORGANIZATION AND RECRUITMENT OF CREWS

Men who are members of the same crew refer to each other as *camaradas,* and are described as *companheiros*. Both terms imply a measure of *ésprit de corps* and fellowship. In actual fact, however, they do not form real corporate groups that in any way might be compared to the lineages. A distinction, however, must be drawn between the diminutive crews of the *lanchas* and those of the larger vessels. If these small crews display a larger measure of corporateness than those of the *candis, botes* and *rapas,* it is because they often are formed by small family groups—father and son, brothers, nephews, and in-laws. The corporate nature of these small groups does not derive from the fact that they belong to the same crew, but rather they belong to same crew because they belong the same lineage or connected lineages.

A *crew,* camaradas, *returning from the sea. The fellowship of the crew members cannot compete with the corporateness of groups based on the family. (from the new harbor)*

Larger crews are ephemeral groups with little significance outside the context of fishing. Certain crews demonstrate a larger degree of stability than others, but stability appears to correlate with the success of the enterprise and be determined by convenience rather than by fellowship and loyalty. When crew members choose to remain with the same *mestre* for longer periods, it is because of the prospect of continuing in sharing bigger catches.

Although the fishermen clearly are not workers in the usual sense of the term, they do participate in what only can be called a labor market. In this market the sellers and buyers of labor are not pitted against each other over remuneration and working hours. The crew members compete over opportunities determined by luck or fishing acumen, and the owners over skill, personality, and general performance. In this market there is little scope for corporate action. The common fishermen compete with each other for the most lucrative positions and the *mestres* for the most able men. The negotiations in this market are not straightforward and businesslike, but take place behind a front of vicarious arguments, and an idiom of personal, sometimes emotional reactions. Neither the hard economic facts nor their estimates of performance come out in the open.

The Nazarenos subscribe to an egalitarian ideology, and when the issue was raised among a group of fishermen working with their nets on the beach, it was maintained that all *camaradas* were equal. If some fishermen were more popular with the *mestres,* it was because they were *engraixadores,* flatterers. In private conversations, however, it was admitted that there were indeed great differences between the common fishermen. Some were reliable, sober, and clever in the execution of their duties at sea, others were not. Of particular importance is personality: men who are prone to quarrel and be uncooperative were not appreciated either by their *camaradas* nor their *mestres,* and were described as revolutionaries.

A *mestre* who is dissatisfied with a member of his crew will normally not dismiss him in a straightforward way. Rather he will offend and humiliate him in front of others. This treatment may not always be meant to carry the message of a dismissal, but be due to the nervous tension proper to the fishing activities themselves. *Mestres* are expected to be tense *(cheio de nervos)* on these occasions. But if a crew member is subjected to this behavior several times, his honor demands that he ask for his *cédula,* the certificate issued by the *Capitania,* the fishing authorities, which authorizes its holder to fish in the waters of Nazaré. This document is deposited with the *mestre* when a fisherman joins a crew. A man who asks for his *cédula* is actually resigning from the crew. A crew member who wants to resign on his own account will either provoke an incident, or interpret a remark or a piece of behavior as a sign of being out of favor whether intended or not, and then ask for the *cédula.*

It is regarded as below the dignity of the *mestre* to plead with a *camarada* who has decided to resign. If he did not actually mean to dismiss a man with his intemperate outbursts, he does have ways of showing this without appearing to be actually pleading. Although the reason behind the resignation clearly relates to the poor performance of an enterprise, it will be made to appear as springing from a personal conflict. It is also beneath the dignity of a *mestre* to solicit crew for his boat. He expects to be approached by interested parties or by their representatives. This is not to say that there are no manipulations behind the scenes. The process of recruitment is actually in many cases in the hands of the women, who either will approach the *mestre* directly or through a relation or a friend. This process of recruitment goes on all the time.

The reputations both of the *mestres* and the fishermen are under a more or less constant process of evaluation. The reputation of the *mestre* is based solidly on the catch of his enterprise, and is only marginally affected by his personality and the way he treats the *camaradas*. However, the fishermen's reputation is based on less measurable criteria. Although an able master will have no problems judging his men, his judgment is not based on the solid measures of the catch, and is therefore more difficult to monitor. His judgment is therefore easily disputed. A man who has been dismissed will never see this as based on sound judgment, but as the result of unreasonableness or intrigue.

It is in the obvious interest both of the *mestre* and the fishermen to be in demand. This is reflected in the role-play of the fishermen as well as the general atmosphere that surrounds the process of recruitment. This explains one of the most characteristic features of the personalities of the fishermen: their sensitivity and pride. Often, it seems as if they seize on the slightest reason to be offended and declare that they will never again speak to their offender. These impatient reactions, however, should not always be taken at face value. In order to appreciate a reaction of this sort, it must be known in its full context.

The degree to which men are in demand is essential for their prospects both as fishermen and as *mestres*. Because of the structure of the market, all men are in a certain way in competition with each other. Because of the nature of their enterprise, independence is more important than solidarity. The catch of fish is limited goods after the fact. Before the catch is brought ashore, one man's success is not made at the expense of the other's failure, but is a function of the fickle nature of luck, which cannot be domesticated by any measure of solidarity.

Because few men actually are in urgent demand, playing hard to get becomes a common game. Since a pledge never again to talk to someone rarely is honored, it must be understood as a move in a game of brinkmanship to increase one's personal value rather than a seriously entertained wish to end a relationship.

MESTRES AND COMPANHEIROS

The more successful a master is, the more authority he will be able to exert without losing his crew. The authority of the master is recognized as essential. "A boat is no better than its master" is a common saying. At the spur of the moment, a master may overshoot his mark and drive a *companheiro* into a soul-searching debate between his pride and his needs:

> Last week the boat was fuelling. Zé Júlio was busy washing the deck. By mistake some water came into the fuel tank, and the *mestre* Raba Coelho [a nickname] started to shout at him: "You are only here to annoy me. Go away. Nobody will miss you. You must pay the diesel oil *(gasóleo)* yourself." This week when they were pulling in the traps for crabs and lobster, the rope came into the propeller. They had to do a lot of maneuvring, and in the end had to cut the rope to get it out. Raba Coelho, very angry *(cheio do nervos)*, started to shout to Zé Júlio again, and told him he should have pulled faster. "Get out of my way, you are only making trouble. One day it is the diesel oil, now it is the rope. I will pay you not to go to sea."

Before he went ashore, Zé Júlio asked for his *cédula*. Raba Coelho said O.K., but laughed apologetically. Later he called Zé and asked if he had another place to work. He said no, and Raba Coelho replied: "Where are you going now? Don't do it. You have many children. If you really want to quit, I shall keep you until you have found something else. A man must have a reason, he must think and not provoke me all the time."

Next day Zé Júlio did not join the crew, assuming that they would not go to sea because of the wind. This gave him the opportunity to stay away without making the final decision to quit, somehow making up for the offense. But so far he had not seen any of his *camaradas,* which he normally would have done if they were still ashore. His staying away thus had become more fateful than originally intended. "Now," he complained, "Raba Coelho will believe that I really am quitting." He was suffering visibly, afraid to lose his job on one of the most successful boats of Nazaré, one which earned at least 300.000$ for each *camarada* annually.

Raba Coelho is known as one of the most forceful *mestres* of the *praia*, feared and respected. Zé Júlio is a fisherman of good standing, who neither drinks nor shirks his work. The incident should therefore be dismissed as a conspiracy of unfortunate circumstances. Raba Coelho did not want to get rid of Zé, but was carried away by his temperament, and Zé did not want to quit, but had to take action to protect his dignity. Raba Coelho really solved the case by discreetly repenting his rashness. Now another circumstance threatened to make final an act that was merely intended as a demonstration. But Zé Júlio in the end kept his place as a *companheiro* of Raba Coelho.

Incidents of a similar sort may have a different outcome, as the case of the less successful *mestre* Lázaro shows. When in the process of casting the net, the *mestre* told a member of the crew to let go of the float, but the man did not hear. Lázaro shouted at him and called him a variety of unpleasant names. Another of the *companheiros* defended the unfortunate *camarada*, and got himself a tongue lashing too. When they hauled the net, they got 25 crates of *carapau*, a most successful catch. In spite of this the two men asked for the *cédula* when they reached the shore. Another young fisherman quit shortly afterwards. These events were revealed during an evening at the northern wall of the esplanade, popularly referred as *Muro da Crítica, Muro da Censura,* or *Muro da Vergonha,* the unofficial debating forum of the fishermen. The three men did not spare the skipper, who was not present, and one of them declared that he would rather eat rotten apples than go to sea with Lázaro.

A critical discussion of the nature of the *mestres* followed. One of the great masters, Armando São Brás, also became the target of criticism because five months before, he dismissed 11 *companheiros* when he changed from line- to net-fishing, no doubt a postponed outcome of the famous strike. He only kept five crew members, and these five were duly characterized as *engraixadores*, flatterers, an epithet often invoked in usually abortive attempts to create a common front among the *camaradas*. When they fail it is because a fisherman would rather bear this calumny than risk his position on a successful enterprise.

A number of the masters were criticized because they were regarded as superior and aloof. A *mestre* is regarded as superior if he does not associate with his *camaradas* ashore. Not surprisingly, the masters regarded as the most aloof and superior were those who were the most successful, *os Campeões,* Armando São Brás, João Álvaro, Alhinha, and a few others.

One of the more popular masters was Américo. He was described as a man of calmness and composition. But he had one defect: he would remain at sea longer than his *companheiros* wanted. Once the crew-members from Sítio complained that they would not reach the *elevador*, the tram, from Nazaré if they remained at sea much longer. In spite of this Américo insisted that they cast the net once more, and the men had to ascend to Sítio by night on foot. But Américo did not associate exclusively with the other *mestres* and was moderately successful.

In a discussion on the relationship between the *mestres* and the *companheiros,* Raba Coelho complained that he had heard that some members of his crew wanted to give him hell:

Not infrequently the crew-members accuse the masters of being thieves, exploiters and fascists. This is because they have not made the sacrifices and taken the risks the *mestres* have made in order to get their boats and equipment.

He had himself been exposed to the dangers of *Gronelândia* and *Terra Nova* on *bacalhau*-fishing in order to save money. At times, he hardly had clothes to wear because he saved everything for his boat. "The problem in Nazaré is above all the envy, *inveja*," he said. "If you earn more than 500$ they will start to denigrate you *(denegrir)*." In spite of this he enjoyed the company of his *companheiros:*

> You do not lose your respect because you associate with your crew. The crucial thing is that a master must have a strong personality, *uma personalidade mais forte*. And he must not get drunk so he will keep his authority if one of his *companheiros* dares to come on board in that deplorable condition.

In spite of his assurance of enjoying the company of his crew, he declared that a certain reserve must be kept between the *mestre* and his *companheiros*. Under no conditions must he let anyone diminish his personality *(manter uma reserva entre o mestre e os companheiros—nao deixar diminuir a personalidade)*. Raba Coelho had resolved the problem of authority by keeping himself in splendid isolation. He was never to be seen in the *tabernas*, not even in those where the *mestres* congregated.

Armando São Brás, who is particularly mentioned as a *mestre* who only associated with other masters, also claimed that envy was the big problem in Nazaré. He confirmed that he did not associate much with his *companheiros*. But he maintained that it was different before the strike of 1974. Before the strike he would often eat with his crew, but he had been terribly offended during the strike, having been accused of being a thief and a fascist. He even got engaged in a fistfight. On the *praia*, the beach, which is shorthand for the community of Nazarenos, there were only people who wished him all manner of evil. Therefore he rarely visited the *tabernas*, and preferred to associate with people from outside. Rather than going to the *tabernas*, he would visit the cafes, the habitat of the bourgeoisie.

In spite of the fact that some of the successful masters associate with the bourgeoisie, it is not a question of *aburguesamento*. The *mestres* do not aspire to become members of the bourgeoisie with all that implies about a change of manners and orientation. The relationship is more in the nature of patron-client, often sealed by common meals, excursions, and bacchanals. The masters gain potential allies in a world that otherwise remains closed to them, and also seem to gain some satisfaction and prestige by associating with the so-called *gente boa* (good people). Although these relationships with the bourgeoisie are criticized and envied, an accomplished master will not be accused of being an *exgraixador* when associating with *gente boa*, which would invariably be the case of a fisherman of lesser distinction. This, incidentally, proved to be a big obstacle to the full participation of the anthropologist in the community of the fishermen. In spite of genuine efforts to part with a northern-European identity, I was for several months persistently classified as *Francês*, which is synonymous with a foreign bourgeois tourist. My promotion to the rank of honorary Nazareno was achieved when one of the great *mestres*, Isidro Meca, accepted me as a member of his entourage of *burgueses*, lesser *mestres* and selected members of his crew. The process of initiation, as briefly mentioned earlier, had the form of a glorious bacchanal, and concluded with a parade through the narrow streets of Nazaré, with my protector in visible high spirits.

My protector was a *mestre* of unique qualities both as a fisherman and as a human being. He had for several years been one of the acknowledged leaders in the profession, "a champion of fishing." He was a man of strong personality, and unusual intelligence and orientation. He was completely sovereign in his manners and style of life. No adherent of the high principles of Raba Coelho, he was a heavy drinker who even when under the sway of a generous measure of liquor never lost his dignity and self-control. He was also a very hard worker, always busy with his various enterprises, bristling with energy and good spirits.

Isidro Meca was the most clearcut example of the charismatic basis of the biggest and most successful fishing enterprises in Nazaré. As a member of his crew I was in the position to study his style of leadership at a close range. During crucial operations of fishing he made a great show of leadership with his intense participation and undisputed command, often impatient and demanding. He had no patience with crew members who were giving less than 100 percent attention and effort, and did not hesitate to dismiss his own son from the job as *motorista* when he was not up to the mark.

It is maintained that *companheiros* will remain on the average of two years with the same enterprise. This man's turnover was much less, and he had no problems in recruiting new crew members when needed. As long as a *mestre* is a top performer, he is able to dismiss and recruit *companheiros* without difficulty. But if his luck seems to fail, he will start losing his best men. If crew members of their own choice ask for their *cédula* because of minor provocations, it must be regarded as an ominous sign for the *mestre*. An unlucky *mestre* who starts losing his best men is certainly not improving his chances of turning his luck.

Some *mestres* seem to have swallowed most of their pride and are willing to accept the most ill-reputed revolutionaries as crew members. This was the case with Pé-de-Burro (Donkey foot), who heads a most miserable team of alcoholics and assumed drug addicts. He is probably at the bottom rung of the Nazaré enterprises, which are unofficially graded on a scale according to performance and prestige.

In spite of its informal nature, the labor market on the *praia* establishes an efficient system of "prices" that distinguishes between the quality of men and *mestres*. The game of playing hard to get can be seen as a manner of salesmanship on the labor market. The selection takes place without official reference to the "prices," i.e., the reputation of the *mestres,* in an idiom of personal relationships.

A woman who is soliciting for a job for her husband or son will primarily try to find personal connections in the network that connects the appropriate lineages. She will not offend the egalitarian ideology by emphasizing the particular merits of the man, but will obliquely invoke the appropriate relationship in order to promote her case. Sometimes a successful master may be persuaded to take on an ill-reputed relative, but in general the decisions, masked by a polite form and good excuses, appear to be hard-headed and rational.

During my fieldwork it was actually a seller's market. There were opportunities even for those of the most tarnished reputations, but only in the lowest performing enterprises. At the same time, *mestres* on the lookout for a decent crew could have serious problems. The *rapa Porto do Abrigo* remained idle for lack of a crew the *mestre* César could accept. César could be seen pacing the esplanade in a somber mood. When approached, he complained that his luck had failed him for no obvious reason. For several years he had performed decently, sometimes even better than Armando São Brás. It was not because he did not know the sea and his craft. He maintained that his knowledge in certain respects was better than that of São Brás. "I don't know why the luck failed me," he said. "I don't have a bad soul *(um mau íntimo)*, and I don't know why people should be envious of me!" This statement reveals that he suspected that his bad luck was caused by the ill will of other Nazarenos. "I have followed the advice of these women [he avoided the word *bruxa*], but my luck failed me just the same," he said.

His problem peaked when the motor failed during the *carapau* season. He asked his brother-in-law, who worked as machinist, to fix it. He refused and asked for his *cédula,* and the rest of the crew did the same. He blamed his brother-in-law, whom he maintained influenced the other *companheiros*. This happened at the top of the season when many other boats were making a lot of money. This fact naturally increased the frustration of his men. He took some comfort from the fact that the same had happened to other *mestres,* like Zé Barata, Zé Robalo, and the son of Sargo. He explained that the *mestres* were the main victims of envy. But if he succeeded in recruiting a crew, he would continue fishing. If not, he would sell his boat and find something to do ashore.

When asked why he did not actively try to recruit a crew, his reply was, "I have been here a long time, it has never been my way to ask people to work for me. I am here in front of the sea, everybody knows my situation. If they want, they can come and talk to me."

César was seen walking the esplanade for several days, probably hoping that someone would approach him. But in the end he had to give up. He sold his boat. But rather than finding a land-based job, he joined one of the *candis* as a crew member. Although he would have been able to recruit some of the more notorious elements of the *praia,* his dignity prevented him from doing so.

THE INDIVIDUAL AND THE CREW

Although fishing is the *raison d'être* of Nazaré, the organization of the fishing enterprises as such has failed to create groups with any measure of corporate strength. The crews are really ad hoc groups of men, each of whom is pursuing his own separate career. If a better opportunity is found with a different crew, no loyalty is expected; job changes are natural, and made without reproach or criticism. This lack of corporateness is clearly demonstrated at sea. Each *companheiro* brings his own food, formerly in the gaily painted wooden *fóquim,* nowadays in less colorful tin boxes. There is no sharing of food, nor even a fixed time for a meal. Each crew member will eat when he feels hungry and the situation makes it possible.

There is a conspicuous lack of conviviality. Each fisherman is a rugged individualist. Sometimes the *mestre* will pass a keg of wine around, as one of the few expressions of togetherness. After reaching the fishing ground, the pursuit of fish requires an input of labor and attention that excludes socializing. Only when back on the shore with the catch will the crew sometimes make a joint meal, the famous *caldeirada*. (The *caldeirada*, prepared in a large pan, as the name implies, consists of a choice selection of fish from the catch, boiled with onions, potatoes, vegetables, and spices.) It must be stressed, however, that bonds of togetherness and sympathy *are* created among these men who struggle together, are exposed to the dangers at sea under the same leadership, and share in the fortune of their enterprise. Possibly what exists of *ésprit de corps* seems to be rather subdued because the crews embarking together on the shore of Nazaré superficially appear as a primordial example of male togetherness.

The *tabernas* are not perceived as a locus of interaction for the crews. Neighborhood and lineage ties are probably more important. The relationship between men outside the more intimate sphere of the lineage appears to be guided more by interest than by feeling. Although communality dominates almost completely, pleas are sometimes made for a special, dyadic friendship relation. But in my experience these were made mainly to solicit special favors. Sometimes a friend of the moment feels called upon to warn against the cynic designs of other possible rivals to the friendship. This demonstrates that the idea of friendship is poorly developed but not entirely absent.

One cannot help being surprised by the naivety of these friendship declarations, and the lack of insight in interpersonal relations that are revealed from time to time. One likely explanation is that the communal nature of social relations in Nazaré does not promote proficiency in role switching, which seems necessary in order to take an outside view of one's own performance, a *sine qua non* for a sophisticated insight into social relationships. That is not to say that insight of this order is absent in Nazaré, only that a particular kind of naivety seems to be fairly widespread. Characteristic of this naivety is also a strong demand for consistency in behavior and opinion. Yet complete consistency in the management of social relations in Nazaré is by no means a simple matter. It could well imply either an intolerable degree of tactlessness or the isolation of a hermit. For example, a man will accuse a friend of being false *(falso)* if he is caught in an encounter with someone with whom the man himself is not on speaking terms at the moment.

The best way of avoiding the onus of such accusations is to commit yourself as little as possible. For good reasons, the Nazarenos will warn you against showing too much confidence *(confiança)* in your fellow men in general. The social organization of Nazaré does not facilitate the exclusive type of friendship characteristic of the middle class (Paine 1969). Once when I asked a young man who his best friend was, he remained silent for a long time and finally replied, "My brother."

For the individual fisherman, his crew companions are of importance as a peer group because his remuneration relates also directly to his membership status in the crew. On the other hand, beyond this there is very little of interpersonal dependency in this group. Every fisherman is concerned with his reputation, but no single personal relationship can be held responsible for his standing on the *praia*.

Although individual cases of slander are detected and punished, the opinion of hundreds of fishermen is beyond the power of single persons or even a coordinated group of persons.

This attitude, characteristic of the men of the *praia,* was illustrated in a particularly pictureque way by an elderly fisherman of a somewhat philosophical disposition:

> When we look at the sky during the night, we can see some isolated stars and other stars in groups. The lonely star is good, and is the star of a good man on this earth. Every human being has his star. The stars in groups are the stars of those men on this earth who join together to gossip [*falar mal*] about the others.

The individual man, in terms of reputation, is pitched against a multitude of persons belonging to the same community as himself. It is the psychological impact of faceless corporations, yet consists of people with whom he is likely to have personal relationships of some sort, which facilitates beliefs in spirit aggression (Brøgger 1986).

The Nazarenos subscribe to beliefs in witchcraft and sorcery as well as spirit aggression, and, as we have seen in the two preceding chapters, the social organization of the *praia* provides precisely the kind of experiences that tend to make these beliefs into explanatory theories with regard to disease, misfortune, and destiny.

The following chapters explore these beliefs in more detail.

6 / Supernatural Beliefs and Reason in the Pursuit of Fish

We have so far been mainly concerned with how beliefs relate to the structure of relationships. In this chapter we shall consider how experiences inherent in the pursuit of fish are to be understood.

Fishing is dependent upon luck, much as agriculture is dependent upon fertility. But where the mysteries of fertility are more or less controlled by the science and technology of modern agriculture, fishing is not completely under rational control, and may never be. In spite of echosounders and other scientific equipment, the success of Nazareno fishermen seems to depend on luck as much as ever before.

In order to demonstrate how luck is perceived among the Nazarenos, we shall first examine the effects of the big catch and then investigate their interpretation of luck. It appears that both supernatural and rational explanations prevail. The importance of knowledge and experience is clearly recognized, but in many ways they fail as explanation. In these cases, supernatural explanations are invoked. It is our concern in this chapter to demonstrate how these relate to the structure of relationships at sea.

One of the hard facts of life for the men of the *praia* is the conspicuous differences in the size of the catch between similar enterprises. One fisherman maintains that fishing is like the lottery: everybody cannot win the same throw. At closer range, however, it appears that fishing is not quite a lottery as the man says. The big prizes are not randomly distributed. Some men are persistent winners. This shows that there is more to it than mere chance. But it also occurs that winners turn losers, as the case of César demonstrates.

The unpredictable nature of luck provides fishing with its unique fascination. Even a weak performer sometimes makes a big catch, an event that nourishes secret hope that he one day will really make it. It is this pattern of intermittent reinforcement that lends to fishing some of the psychological appeal of gambling.

THE BIG CATCH

Hope is nourished by the windfall catch an enterprise may occasionally make. A particular example is that of João Álvaro:

One morning the *rapa* of João Álvaro could be observed in front of the auction hall *(a lota)* in the southern end of Nazaré, heavily loaded with fish. His boat

The horns tied to the mast of a modern vessel protect against the evil eye. (from the new harbor)

was so heavy that only the generosity of the weather and the sea kept it from capsizing. Soon after sunrise the *praia* was buzzing with rumors of the catch of the year, which was said to be worth more than 10 million escudos, a whole year's income for a moderately successful *rapa*. It appeared that the rumors for a change were not exaggerated. João Álvaro had made a fabulous catch of *rubalo,* one of the highest priced species, which on this day commanded a price of 480 escudos per kilogram.

Several *candis* brought load after load ashore without visibly relieving the loaded vessel. An old enormous transport vessel, *Maria Eulália,* which had been idle since the day of the big trawlers, was hauled to sea. Wholesalers from Peniche arrived with trucks to compete with the local *peixeiras* (fish-sellers) for the catch, which helped to stabilize the price somewhat. The unloading took many hours.

Wherever Nazarenos congregated that day, the only theme of discussion was the marvelous catch of João Álvaro. Although no one could deny him the luster of a hero, the famous *inveja* (envy) of the *praia* did not fail to materialize. The first reactions of the wife of one of the leading "champions" was, "If João Álvaro has any sense of shame, he should not go to sea for a while so his exhausted crew will have time to rest." Her daughter later made the following contribution to the gossip of the street: "I have heard that the catch is due to a trick João Álvaro made. All the fish were in the net of Zé da Camila, but the net burst and the whole catch went into the hands of João Álvaro."

She also said that João Álvaro had played the same trick on a *retornado* (a man returned from the lost African colonies). Rumor had it that the *retornado* had made an official complaint with the commander of the *Capitania.* At this juncture her

father turned up and she exclaimed: "Do you know that João Álvaro has made a catch worth ten millions?" "Don't make me angry" *(não me chateises)* was his immediate reaction.

The wife of another *mestre,* O Borracha, complained that they had a crew of desperately poor *companheiros,* and never did they have such luck like this.

Another woman replied that it had always been like this. When she was young, there were nets that got a lot and others nothing. Money wants money, she said. The case of João Álvaro clearly confirmed this, because not long ago he had made a catch of 1.2 million, which was regarded as enormous. Even Vasco's catch of 600,000 was regarded as extraordinary. Now João Álvaro had beaten his former record almost ten times, although some of the other masters maintained that the catch probably did not exceed five million.

The long face of the year belonged to one of João Álvaro's *companheiros,* who left the crew a few days before because of a minor disagreement. His situation now served as a memento to *companheiros* in general not to quit a successful enterprise. One woman maintained that João Álvaro was evil because he would block out his lights so as not to reveal to the others the places with a lot of fish. But another woman came to his defense and claimed that was normal behavior. "If your father got hold of a shoal of fish," she said, "would he tell all the others where he got it?" Hers was a lonely voice, however. The general reaction of the *praia* proved the old saying that no man can become a prophet in his own town.

Some days later, a story circulated to the effect that João Álvaro had cast his net the moment he saw that the catch escaped Zé de Camila. But in this story the escape was not due to the tricks of João Álvaro, but was an act of destiny. When Zé saw his big catch, he became proud *(commençou a soberbar)* and observed that there were certain persons in Nazaré he would not give as much as one *robalo.* At this, his net burst. The actual facts as told by the son of Zé de Camila, however, were the following: The boat of Zé de Camila, *Novo Leonor José,* at first cast net outside São Pedro and after that went northwest. Just outside the lighthouse the echosounder picked up strange signals, and they prepared for the next try. As the same time João Álvaro came in from the west with *Novo Estrelinha* and asked if they had got any fish. They told him that they had caught some *carapau* on their first try. At that time the *Novo Estrelinha* picked up the same signals and immediately cast the net in a circle. Shortly afterwards, Zé de Camila did the same. João Álvaro, however, managed to surround almost the whole shoal and Zé only caught 19 *robalos.* His judgment was that João Álvaro had done nothing wrong. But if he had not seen *Novo Leonor José,* he would not have come, because there are rarely fish in these waters. The big catch of João Álvaro, however, not only provoked envy, but also nourished the hopes most fishermen entertain of one day making the big catch, thus dramatically illustrating the effects of intermittent reinforcement.

THE NATURE OF LUCK

Novo Estrelinha's fabulous catch provoked discussions of why some fishermen have luck, others not. Every fisherman without exception regarded luck as essential. Several of the men maintained that there could be no luck without knowledge and hard work, but a substantial number of men would not dismiss supernatural forces. Of 20 *mestres* who were interviewed, 11 stated that they did not believe that supernatural forces could influence the outcome of fishing. Among the 11, five had actually consulted *bruxas,* witches, in order to improve their performance. It is significant that only a small minority of these were willing to admit that *inveja*, envy, as an independent force could affect their luck. One of them said, "There are people who really are evil and who nourish evil wishes against men with luck. It is this aggression [*raiva*] which can truly hurt." Another told the following story:

> When I was working on a *traineira* in Matosinhos, the witch, *bruxa*, came on board. The *bruxa* in Matosinhos told everyone to be under deck when she came on board. No one was allowed to be near her as she said her prayers and put a pan [*telhado*] with burning charcoal in the *pejada* [where the fish is stored]. Shortly afterwards we caught a lot of fish.
>
> In Nazaré the *bruxa* will not come on board to bless the boat. People have to come to her and explain what has happened, and she will explain what to do to fight the evil. In one way or another, this gives results. It is the hate of people [*má-fé*] which destroys. There is a woman who has the evil eye [*malolhado*]. When she is looking at a creature [*criatura*] that creates a terrible evil power [*feitiço*]. That can destroy the life of a person. It is a gift of some people to be able to do evil with their eyes and make people sick.
>
> The only defense a person has to divert this *feitiço* is the witch. She will immediately find out what is wrong. I don't know from where the witches get their gift of power. When we go to a witch if our fishing is not successful, it always changes for the better. If it does not happen immediately, it works after some time.

A mestre of *rede do arrasto* (a reference to the equipment of *arte xávega*) told the following story to explain his belief:

> "Often when they are afraid of the evils of envy, *mal d'inveja*, the fishermen will consult a witch. On other occasions at sea when things do not turn out as they should, it is because *Fulano* or *Sircano* [i.e., someone] has provoked a *praga* [*rogou uma praga*]. They will then visit the witch. This with witches is a reality [*mas isto de bruxas e uma realidade*]. Once the wife of Emilio Salvador, who is the partner of my father, came to my mother's house. During their conversation she discovered a *terrine* of porcelain which my mother had. "Oh, what a nice *terrine*, oh my sister-in-law," she exclaimed. And the woman gazed at the thing with such an intensity that it burst. Oh, *comadre*, my mother was unable to speak and the little woman went to the witch. The witch knew what had happened without being told. It is true. The woman who came into the house had also bewitched our net [*enfeitiçado*]. It happened more than once that we could see the fish in the sack of the net, but when we got it ashore, it was empty. [His wife, who was present, nodded.] It was this woman who had hit the net with the evil eye and made the net burst. It is indeed true [*era tudo verdade*]. The witch arranged to have the net smoked [*defumadores*], and the ashes had to be thrown at sea. "Next time you throw the net, you will have a sack full of *carapau*," the witch told us. And it was true.

It must be admitted that the story above has the ring of a fairytale, and it should be mentioned that Ti Francisco (Uncle Francisco, the normal term of reference and address of older men of the *praia*) enjoyed telling the story and probably was more concerned with its entertainment value than its veracity.

If we consider the development of European folklore in recent centuries, we find the beliefs of one generation have become the fairytales of the next. Yet, beyond doubt, beliefs in supernatural forces are seriously entertained by a substantial majority of the *praia*. But as we shall see, the greatest "champions" of the *mestres* of Nazaré readily dismiss supernatural forces. It is common knowledge, however, that their wives consult the witches of the *praia*. Even the skeptics among the men had a less than firm commitment to the world view of modern reason. The conversation with Ti Zé Barata, who lost his boat because of poor catches, probably reveals the basic attitude of the skeptics.

"What is the reason for success in fishing?" I asked.

"Sometimes it is luck, sometimes knowledge [*prática*]. There are some that are born with luck, others without. My boat arrived at the same time as that of Armando São Brás. But today I am without my boat. He has always been a man of luck—he was and he is. But of course, he also has knowledge. But I also have knowledge, but at a certain time the fish disappeared for me. I was fishing near the others, they came in heavy with fish, and I, nothing."

"Do you know any reason for this lack of success?"

"To this day I have no idea of why."

"Do you not know the sea and the techniques of fishing?"

"Of course I know. But sometimes luck refuses to protect us."

"Did you something to improve your luck?"

"Many times my wife went to the witch, but I do not believe in any of this. I only believe that there is something which dominates us, all the rest is imagination [*tretas*]. Sometimes I came from the sea with some fish, and my wife would say, 'Oh, Zé, today I was in that house' [the common reference to the witches is *éstas casas,* these houses]. I replied, 'Is it because you went to the witch that I caught some fish today?' Perhaps the witch was with me on board. I made myself a skeptic, but to tell the truth, when she went to the witch, I did get some fish."

Although only three of the *mestres* interviewed admitted that they believed that the feeling of envy alone could affect the performance of a fisherman, another seven believed that luck could be affected by supernatural procedures. That is to say, they were more inclined to believe in sorcery than in witchcraft as defined by the criteria of E. E. Evans-Pritchard (1937). Even one of the great champions of the *mestres* admitted that he feared the forces of *pragas*.

SORCERY AND SPIRIT AGGRESSION

The *pragas* represent a particular form of sorcery with obvious roots in traditional European witch-beliefs. It may be mentioned in passing that these beliefs technically speaking consist of a combination of beliefs in sorcery and spirit-aggression. The witches were believed to use a variety of substances, rust from church-bells, bile from toads, snake skin, and other matters of sordid provenance, to work their alchemy of evil. But equally important were prayers and incantations through which the assistance of the devil himself was enlisted.

In the Nazareno beliefs, the enlistment of the devil and the manipulations of "medicines" do not always go together. In order to invoke the *pragas,* a spiritual ritual alone is necessary. This ritual is on the one hand believed to enlist the occult power of the sun, and, on the other, the devil. The role of the sun, which sometimes is referred to as *o sol divino,* invites speculations of pre-Christian origins for this element of belief. The belief in the role of the devil is solidly within the European tradition of folk religion.

Apart from the "powers" already mentioned, there is also a general belief in spirits. Most of them are believed to be spirits of known and unknown deceased human beings who for various reasons have not been accepted into the divine realm of heaven. But there are also spirits of unknown provenance, commonly referred to as *entidades,* which appear to be small independently operating devils. An elderly woman who is regarded as somewhat eccentric and feared by the fishermen because she sometimes can be seen in the process of performing the dreaded ritual explains: "People invoke *pragas* [*rogem pragas*] because they want to hurt others. In order to do this, they appeal to the divine sun to take charge. In order to make the *praga* efficient, they must pray at sunrise, sunset, or at midday, or even more efficiently, between the blessing of the bread and wine during mass [*entre a hóstia e o Santissima*]."

In order to invoke *pragas* against the owners of the boats so they will lose their luck, the following incantation must be presented:

Pela luz que nos ilumina
Tanto peixe . . .
que não ganhasses
um tostão

By the light that illuminates us
No matter how much fish you catch
may you never earn a cent

If not in church, the person should get on his knees facing the sun and raise closed eyes against the sun while mumbling the incantation. The following case presented by the prominent *peixeira* (fish-seller) Maria Cândida illustrates both the effects of *pragas* and how they may be lifted:

My brother-in-law had many problems in his life. He had problems with the engine of his boat which cost him seventy thousand and which kept the boat ashore for more than three weeks. One *lancha* went to the bottom. Because my sister is very fond of money (and therefore could be suspected of not consulting a witch simply to save money), I went to a witch with my sisters Clara and Júlia.

The old witch had passed away, and the daughter who followed in her footsteps, explained that she did not have the same gift *(condão)* as her mother, but asked them to present their problem. Maria Cândida explained that her brother-in-law was completely bound *(enleado):* "He is so out of his mind that he does not sleep in his bed, but remains on the sofa and sleeps on the floor." The witch then fetched a plate with oil and water. She made signs of the cross above the plate and said some prayers. Then she said, "He is full of *pragas,* he has the Enemy [the devil] on board his boat." She looked to heaven to ask the *Madrinha* (the dead witch) to liberate this brother from the pains he suffered in the grip of the enemy. She also invoked the assistance of São Vicente and Santo Padre Cruz with such an intensity of conviction that both Maria Cândida and her sisters started crying. Maria Cândida had brought some bits of the fishing equipment, a shred of her brother-in-law's clothes, a handkerchief and a photograph of the owner of the boat. "The witch kept these pieces and asked us to smoke the boat *(fumar),* gave us holy water and some small sacks of white powder to spread on the sides of the boat." Later Maria Cândida asked a nephew to put the powder on the sides of the boat and gave him a piece of paper with the prayers to be recited during the smoking.

When they returned from the witch, they saw a black entity approaching them: "We exclaimed at the same time: 'Credo, go and burst in the fat sands' [*carede, vai rebentar ás areias gordas*], because we both knew where that one came from. Then I taught my brother-in-law following prayer:

Deus vai comigo
É eu vou com ele.
Deus à minha frente
è eu àtrás dele."

God go with me
and I with him
God in front of me
and I behind him.

She told her brother-in-law to recite this prayer three times before leaving home. After this, the fishing improved.

In these procedures we encounter the well-known repertory of Catholic folk culture where elements from the Church cult in the form of holy water and prayers are mixed with ritual knowledge of unknown, probably of pre-Christian origin.

An affiliation to a genuine ritual tradition is evident in the emphasis on liminality, which refers to the period between states of being, as the period between night and day. When it is neither day nor night, a particular state of liminality prevails. Liminal states are generally believed to be fraught with danger, as in cases of *rites de passage*. When an individual has been cut off from his former state of being, for example, childhood, and before he or she has been incorporated into the community of grownups, a liminal state prevails. Although the concept of liminality is almost universally found in ritual thinking, it is unlikely that it should have been recreated by an eccentric old lady or even by a more accomplished village witch. It is more likely to emerge as an idiom within a comprehensive ritual tradition that has been kept alive by the ritual specialists of European folk culture.

It is my assumption that beliefs are generated within a context of social encounters in which the experience of dependency is crucial. As we have seen, the pursuit of fishing involves personal relationships, first of all to other people within the same enterprise, but also to other *mestres* and crews that jointly provide the standards both of performance and behavior. These relationships are first of all of contractual, yet also of a strongly personal nature. The contracts are not phrased in a judicial idiom, nor depersonalized by bureaucratic formulas through which independent rules beyond the influence of personal sympathies and whims are involved. The mode of perception, as in the case of house contracts, is that of the traditional community, which tends to emphasize personal rather than impersonal forces. The recognition of the objective forces of nature as the dominant forces of destiny is clearly related to urban society, in which limited and instrumental relationships are the rule.

The field of relationships involved in fishing does not promote the ascribed closeness as experienced among tribal lineage mates, yet is personal enough to promote fears of supernatural forces in the form of sorcery. Also, the individual fisherman, with regard to his reputation, is pitched against a multitude of people belonging to the same community as himself, which he cannot get away from. His relationship to the people of the *praia* may be described as ascribed and corporate. This is a situation which should facilitate beliefs in spirit aggression.

Another, although marginal reason, to prefer sorcery explanations to those of witchcraft is that they have an instrumental dimension that is more easily reconciled with the modern world view, with which the Nazarenos are more or less familiar. One elderly fisherman believed that the "medicines" used by sorcerers could be purchased at the local pharmacy. The difference between biochemical effects of certain medicines and the occult effect of the medicines of sorcerers is not obvious for people with no training in the sciences. Another reason to believe in supernatural forces in general is that they provide the losers with a convenient excuse for failure. Not surprisingly, it was the most successful *mestres* who tended primarily to emphasize that luck was not independent of knowledge and experience in the art of fishing.

THE IMPORTANCE OF KNOWLEDGE

In a discussion of the different results of fishing enterprises, Armando São Brás, one of the leading "champions," explained that there are different fishing techniques *(artes)*. The success of an enterprise, he said, is above all dependent upon the knowledge of the master, although he also admitted that a measure of luck was involved. He was positive, however, that envy could not influence the outcome of fishing. Indeed, his own success testified to this, because he was very conscious of all the envy that surrounded him on the *praia*. In fact, the whole *praia* without exception wished that his luck would turn.

One of the main reasons for his own good fortune was that he knew where to look for fish. Fish are not evenly distributed along the fishing grounds of Nazaré. Often he would see *mestres* casting their nets where he knew there would be no fish. These *mestres* would later be the most envious when he returned with a good catch while they were more or less empty-handed. He would not dismiss supernatural forces out of hand, but simply stated that he had never consulted a witch because it had not been necessary.

Ailinha, also one of the "champions," maintained that luck came to those who worked hard. During the interview he was busy repairing his net. He pointed to the net and his tools and explained: "If these had been letters I would have been a professor." He added, "The sea also has its secrets. When we are together with our friends we exchange these secrets. That is information of high value which you only share with a friend." It was understood that he was referring to the small circle of successful *mestres* he associated with.

A young, newly established *mestre* was the most explicit about the importance of knowledge. Luck is important, he said, but it is above all the method that is important, and knowledge of the sea. Certain fishing grounds *(pesqueiros)* had fish only certain periods of the year. He had himself systematized his knowledge in a book, where he indicated the location, the catch, and also the depth. He would also consult some of the old *mestres* who were willing to share their knowledge with

The mending and making of nets and equipment is the most important male pursuit ashore. It provides them with legitimacy and identity in a world dominated by their women.

him. When he was line fishing, he would always try to keep the hooks in the area between rock and sand. Some fishermen will try their luck on the rocks, but they will get nothing.

In order to know the fishing grounds it is important to know the signals *(os sinais)*. The signals consist of various landmarks along the coast. Fertile fishing grounds will be remembered through a complex pattern of landmarks that has to be learned through experience. He had concentrated on these signals from the beginning of his career, but he was not able to remember them in the same way as Joaquim de Teresa, who kept everything in his head and was able to describe them. He himself would recognize the locations on the spot. It is always important to try new areas, although some people remain on the same spot all the time. This is the case of Samora. He will only visit his "little sea" *(maresinho)* and will never become a great fisherman. When trying his luck on new grounds, this young *mestre* will explore the bottom with a sinker smeared with fat. If the sinker reveals that the bottom consists of crude sand *(areia grossa),* he knows that the possibilities are good. If it indicates rock bottom, it will not pay to try his luck.

The *mestre* who was recognized as the most experienced and knowledgeable with regard to the fishing grounds of Nazaré was João Álvaro. He knew the intricate pattern of sand, rock, and vegetation, as well as the invisible channels between various submarine hills. His experience coordinated this knowledge with the temperature, weather, and the condition of the season into expert guesses of where shoals of fish were likely to be found. To the non-initiate, the surface of the sea appears more or less as a monotonous desert of water. Not so for João Álvaro and the other great "champions." They read the sea as an open book, which is meaningless to an unknowledgeable, but exciting and meaningful to the initiate who can read the signs.

Instantly, knowledge combines with a complex pattern of signals and meteorological minutiae into a feeling, at the level of intuition, of where a shoal may be moving and the net may successfully be cast. The ability to absorb and combine this enormous body of knowledge is apparently a rare gift, which explains the charismatic nature of "championship" in Nazaré. João Álvaro obviously knows that his unique command of the art of fishing is not easily matched, even if others may share his knowledge of the fishing grounds. Thus he has generously prepared a detailed map of the local waters that is used by the school of fishing in Nazaré.

The introduction of the echosounder and modern methods of fishing have greatly increased the volume of fish passing the *praia* of Nazaré, but it has not dispelled the beliefs in supernatural forces. In order to change the people of the *praia* into modern rationalists, nothing less than a basic change in the social organization of relationships would be necessary. This is likely to happen only when the traditional folk community is disrupted by the bureaucratic state and the Nazarenos are integrated into an industrial market economy—and their dependence on the lineages and personal relations become less important than their dependence on the social security, banks, and salaried jobs. This development will undoubtedly eventually catch up with Nazaré. Yet in the beginning of the last quarter of the twentieth century, the prebureaucratic community is still alive on the *praia*.

7 / Healing and Belief

Having examined the supernatural beliefs in their different social contexts, a case study of one of the most prominent of the local curers in Nazaré will now be presented. Her various techniques of treatment and her behavior towards her clients will be described. The medieval character of her knowledge and understanding will also be discussed. Finally, an outline of the transformation of this world view with the rise of the urban society and the birth of bourgeois culture will be presented.

The management of the occult forces in Nazaré is solidly in the hands of the women. There are three ritual professional specialists in the village and several minor practitioners. Sometimes they are referred to as *curandeiras,* curers, which is really a correct description of their main efforts. The majority of Nazarenos, however, persist in calling them *bruxas,* witches, a word with sinister overtones of evil. This is probably so because they are generally associated with the same occult forces that the "true witches" supposedly manipulated for their sinister purposes. The average Nazareno's knowledge of these matters is not comprehensive. It is not a dominant feature of their daily life as it is among the Azande (Evans-Pritchard 1937). Yet most Nazarenos do believe that at some juncture of their lives they themselves or their dependents have been exposed to occult forces to a degree that called for professional assistance. The level of supernatural affliction is sufficient to keep several *bruxas* busy in the administration of spells and incantations, and more recently, in an increasing degree, in the communication and management of spirits.

THE MAGIC CURES OF THE LOCAL HEALER

I found that the best way to gather systematic information on these matters was through cooperation with the most prominent of the Nazarena *curandeira* or *bruxa,* Maria Baixinha, who lives modestly in a small apartment, and presents herself as a typical Nazarena. Nothing in her personal appearance reveals her occult powers, nor does her house, its interior decoration and furniture, except for a conspicuous altar dedicated to a number of different saints whom she claims are assisting her in her work. Her main procedure for the treatment of the various ailments brought to her consists of a combination of prayers, sacra, and medicines. Maria makes no clear distinction between holy water, candles from the sacra of the church, traditional folk-medicines, and modern pharmaceutics. She uses camphor and a particular ointment that can be bought without prescription at the local pharmacy. In order to diagnose various ailments, she uses the classical oracle of Mediterranean folk-

The curandeira *(curer) Maria Baixinha at work with a plate of water and olive oil, reciting spells while moving her crucifix. (Photo: Paul Brakgwyn)*

medicine, a plate of water into which are dropped small quantities of olive oil. By the behavior of the drops of oil and the shifting pattern they create on the water's surface, she divines what is causing the ailment or trouble brought to her attention.

No doubt Maria coordinates the observations she makes of her clients with her knowledge of the social life and psychology of the Nazarenos, using the oil-and-water oracle simply to inspire her imagination. Thus it is not a case of fraud; she sincerely believes that the secrets and backgrounds of her clients are revealed in the shifting pattern of olive oil on the water. Some of the ailments brought to her are treated in what we would consider purely medical terms. Some cases of eczema and boils are treated without any investigation into the "patient's" social background and without consultations with the oracle. The application of camphor or ointments, however, is performed with some measure of ritual. Maria usually explains that skin ailments are due to the centipede, *centopeia*. This is not because this insect is particularly common in Nazaré, but probably because of its somewhat sinister appearance. In the case of one child with facial boils, she took a knife and repeatedly made the sign of the cross over the afflicted skin, reciting the following formula:

Eu te corto, coração e corpo
e rabo e cabeça
aranhão e aranhiço
centopeia e centopiço
Em louvour do Senhor São Bento
corte todo o bicho peçonhento
para trás não andarás
e para diante nao adíantarás

I cut you, heart and body
tail and head
scratcher and scratchitcher
centipede and centipeditcher.
In the praise of Saint Benedict
I cut the whole poisonous animal
you will not go backwards
you will not go forwards.

Maria then recited the Lord's Prayer *(Pai Nosso)* and applied an ointment she had bought at the pharmacy. The same cure was repeated three or nine days in a row.

All the other cases were either treated as the result of witchcraft, sorcery, or spirit-aggression. Sometimes one client suffered from a combination of these afflictions. A woman around 40 years of age complained that she was very weak and almost unable to get out of bed in the morning. Maria Baixinha consulted her oracle and came to the conclusion that the woman was suffering from witchcraft, the evil of envy *(mal d'inveja)*, and a spirit who was leaning on her *(encostado)*. Then followed an anamnestic interview that revealed that the spirit bothering her was that of her late mother-in-law. When her mother-in-law was alive, she preferred her daughter. Because of this preference she left nothing to her son, the husband of the afflicted. Her husband now wanted to buy the late mother's house from his sister.

The son of the afflicted had been offered a job in England, but he was never called. Maria explained that a spirit, not identified, was binding him.

Maria again consulted the oil, and saw snakes and eyes. This clearly demonstrated that the woman's life was tied up like a knot *(enleada)*. Maria recited several prayers and massaged the woman with alcohol and camphor, working on the head, behind the ears, and along the back. This was done with movements indicative of driving the affliction out. Maria then took the woman's head between her hands and recited prayers. During these prayers she called on a number of saints and asked in the name of God that the *mal d'inveja, mal olhado* (evil eye) and the *as almas atentadoras* (evil spirits) should go away.

The ritual was repeated the next day. The woman explained that before the treatment day before, a boy, a friend of her son, had been called to England. But after the treatment this boy had become very ill, and her own son had now been called to England in his place. The pajamas of the afflicted boy were now brought to Maria, who doused them with oil and camphor and recited a few prayers. The next day he was reported to have been cured.

After the treatment of the woman, Maria again consulted the oracle. A number of the droplets were moving away from the center, indicating that the evil eye was withdrawing. The previous day she had diagnosed, but not mentioned, that the woman also was hit by a *praga,* but said that was gone now. At the end of the cure the woman was told to smoke her house *(defumadores),* light candles for the saints, and go to mass and pray for the spirits that were bothering her.

When the first woman had left, Maria proceeded to attend her next case. This client, Dona Alice, was afraid of the evil eye because her canary had suddenly died. It is a common belief in Nazaré that occult forces directed against them will often hit the weakest member of a household. To protect their small children, many Nazarenos keep birds to sidetrack the evil. Maria consulted her oracle, and came to the conclusion that it had not been the evil eye, but a *praga* meant for Dona Alice's husband. Maria advised the woman to get a new bird as soon as possible. She pointed at five small drops of oil and identified one of them as the *praga.* She gave the woman the small image of a saint as protection and taught her a prayer, which she solemnly recited:

Eu esperei, o Senhor
Ele inclinou-se para mim
Ouvéu o meu clamor
Inclinou a minhha pedra
Eu ouvi um sopro no çeú
É um vento
Escuta uma voz que te chama
É um convite para longe
Vem comigo
Que eu mando-te esperar.

I waited for the Lord
He approached me
And heard my request
He relieved me from my burden

I heard a breeze in the sky
It is a wind
Listen to the voice that is calling for you
It is an invitation to go far away
Come with me
I am calling for you

Maria repeated the prayer and finally applied ointment and camphor as the day before.

The next case was a mother who brought her three-year-old daughter, who was sick and had lost her appetite. Maria consulted the oracle. The droplets separated on the surface and she concluded that it was a case of the evil of envy. She explained that someone hated the child and that she was envied because she was always nicely dressed. The mother was told to light candles for the *Santíssimo Sacramento* (Holy Sacrament), *Coração Imaculado de Maria* (Mary's Immaculate Heart), *Nossa Senhora do Carmo* (Our Lady of Carmel), and *Sagrado Coração do Jesus* (Holy Heart of Jesus). In addition she was asked to attend a Novena for *Nossa Senhora* (Our Lady). Maria blessed the woman and her child, made the sign of the cross with a crucifix, and applied alcohol and camphor.

For her treatments Maria received the moderate remuneration of a couple of hundred escudos. Clients from very poor families are treated free of charge. Most of her patients are from the community of fishermen in Nazaré, but she is sometimes also consulted by clients from the rural hinterland of Nazaré, which proves that she has an established reputation. During the summer of 1980 she was consulted by a woman whose pig had lost its milk, which threatened the life of a newborn litter. Maria asked the woman to bring her some hairs from the pig, and with her incantations she managed to cure the beast. As remuneration she received one sack of potatoes and one sack of beans.

SPIRITISM AND CURING

The techniques described so far are typical of Mediterranean folk culture, and are, with only minor variations, similar to those found in an Italian peasant community (Brøgger 1971). However, Maria Baixinha has a larger repertory: she performs as a medium in spiritual seances. This is apparently a recent addition to her repertory. It is possible that the communication with spirits through mediums has been introduced by professional spiritists from outside who have established a presence in the village. If that is the case, it is probably a reflection of the spiritist movement that was in vogue and aroused some scientific interest in psychic phenomena in the last quarter of the nineteenth century. Whatever the case, spiritism fits very nicely with the Nazarenos' own spirit beliefs.

As we have seen, there are several kinds of spirits. The most formidable spirit is the devil himself, euphemistically referred to as *Ò Inimigo* or *Tal gaijo* ("the enemy" or "that fellow"). A number of spirits of unknown provenance are referred to as *entidades*. Sometimes these *entidades* reveal themselves as *almas*, souls. These are the souls of dead relatives and friends who return to the community either to help, to say farewell, or to ask for help entering heaven. The belief is that if a person fails to pay a promised contribution to a saint or to the Virgin, he will remain in limbo until the debt has been paid by a relative. Sometimes *almas* from other communities appear because they have failed to get support with their own people. In addition there are master spirits, referred to as *guias*, guides, who are the aids of professional mediums. The most important of these guides is Dr. Sousa Martins, the spirit of a medical doctor from last century who was known for his generous assistance to the poor. There is a cult of Dr. Sousa Martins on the *praia*, and many women have his photograph in their houses and in their pockets.

The Nazarenos are particularly sensitive to the spirits of the dead and they have reason: hardly a year passes without some loss of life at sea. There is an unusual consciousness of death, which is also shared with the children. When people part they will say "See you tomorrow, if God will." It is considered somewhat offensive to take life for granted and therefore a token of dangerous hubris not to add "if God will." To be able to communicate with the souls of people caught by sudden death without warning has a strong appeal to the Nazarenos and is one obvious reason spiritism has become a part of the local culture.

Maria Baixinha's faculties for spiritism seem to have developed in the shadow of the success of the medium Dona Gisela, from the neighboring town of Marinha Grande, whose sessions in Nazaré are recorded as great events. Maria Baixinha's spirit performance became more elaborate and theatrical during the years I had occasion to follow her development. The following case may serve as an example of one of her most impressive performances:

A woman, Marcolina, complained that she suffered from an intractable insomnia. Even if she took sleeping-pills prescribed by the medical doctor, she still remained awake. She would suffer through the night watching the light that was always shining in front of the house altar she kept for the saints. A spirit entered Maria Baixinha and told her that he wanted her to switch off the light in front of the altar: "It is warmer to be close to you when the lights are out, I will not let you sleep unless you turn it off."

Another spirit appeared and started to sing and dance. At this rather dramatic juncture in her performance, I arrived with my assistant. As I entered the room, she grasped her nose as if to blow it and made violent movements with her hands. She became slightly violent and had to be restrained in order not to hit out. Suddenly she was back to normal, greeted me and my companion, and asked if we wanted to assist. Marcolina asked where we came from. When we explained that we came from the house of Santos, whose father was the master of rope-making before the advent of nylon, the woman immediately understood the violent display of Maria. It was the spirit of old Santos, who was known to haunt his old property. Maria explained that I had brought a strong current, *corrente,* to the session. Obviously, the soul of old Santos had followed me in order to get help, because his daughter-in-law did not listen to him. She then complained that she was growing weaker, and she became possessed again. She made the same violent movements with her hands, obviously mimicking the rope-making movements of old Santos.

Marcolina called her: "Ti Maria, Ti Maria."

Maria looked at her with a stern face and repeated angrily: "Ti Maria, Ti Maria." She was obviously impersonating old Santos, and continued the rope pulling movements yelling at some imaginary urchin: *"Sacanas, Sacanas"* (troublemakers). Now Marcolina asked what he wanted. He complained that his family did not help him and he needed light. He assured her that he did not want to hurt anybody.

Maria suddenly changed. She was possessed by a man who had committed suicide, and she made movements as if she wanted to strangle herself. She was restrained, but she managed to take a handkerchief and try to use it as a rope.

The spirit left without revealing its identity and a new spirit, who apparently had died from bronchitis, entered. Maria was breathing with great difficulty. Marcolina asked: "Who are you, what do you want? Are you a good spirit?" Maria nodded, but did not speak. "Can't you talk?" She merely nodded and then withdrew. At last a crying spirit appeared. In a barely audible voice she said, "Oh, my daughter, you are suffering so much." That was the spirit of Maria's deceased mother.

Marcolina tried to comfort her and told her that it was her destiny to help others in their sufferings. Maria continued to cry, and asked Marcolina to kiss her. Obligingly Marcolina gave her many kisses, and the spirit of Maria's mother left. Maria now came to herself, but continued to cry, asking for Dr. Sousa Martins.

While Maria was recuperating from her performance, we asked Marcolina if she was actually haunted by spirits. She denied this, but explained that she had too many worries. Her husband did not get fish and people from her husband's family tried to hurt her. They were envious, and accused her of being conceited *(vaidosa)* and arrogant *(opiniosa)*. A short while before her sister-in-law had invoked *pragas* against her in her very presence.

Maria had by then thoroughly recuperated, and returned to her more traditional arts and consulted the oil-and-water oracle. She could see both Marcolina and her sister-in-law in the oil. But the oil had a somber color, which indicated that Marcolina indeed was having many problems. Both Marcolina and Maria were more comfortable with the oracle and the incantations than with spiritism. But Maria had shown her proficiency as a medium and was therefore ready to compete with Dona Gisela in her home territory.

We went to church and burned a candle for old Santos, discussing the nature of her performance. Her performance was clearly formed on the pattern set by the really accomplished mediums like Dona Gisela from Marinha Grande and Amélia from Peniche. They are willing to perform in front of audiences of more than a dozen clients, all with separate ailments and complaints. A number of different spirits will come forth during these sessions. In some cases the mediums will imitate idiosyncratic features of the people whose spirits they are impersonating, a performance that adds to their credibility. Since Maria Baixinha was performing with a small audience, some of the spirits appeared out of place. The performance was possibly intended as a piece of salesmanship so she could secure for herself a share of the spirit market.

CASES OF LOCAL SPIRITISM

The Nazarenos' belief in spirits is beyond doubt. Sometimes the apparition of spirits takes place under circumstances that may impress even a confirmed skeptic:

When Maria Adélia was around three years of age, her mother heard the child sighing as if possessed by a spirit *(apoquentada)*. The child started to cry and called to her mother for help. She complained that Maximanio was with her. The mother answered that could not be because Maximanio was at home in his own house. The child protested, and said it was another Maximanio, one with a big cap (as the old fishermen can still be seen wearing). This Maximanio had a big nose and he had come to kiss her. The mother understood that it was her husband's uncle, who had recently died and who had been very fond of their daughter. But she cried out to the spirit and said that he had no business in her house. The next morning she poured burned paint on the doorstep to prevent the spirit from entering the house.

The following case happened shortly after the death at sea of five Nazaré fishermen. Four bodies had been recovered from the sea, but Francisco was still missing. After the funeral several women, including her widowed sister-in-law Silvana, a neighbor, and Maria Alzira, my informant, went to the house of Francisco's widow. Sivana fell on the floor and made movements as if she were swimming, and then embraced the widow. They understood that it was Francisco who had come to bid farewell.

Another spirit appeared with the words: "May the peace of the Lord be with you." Maria Alzira asked, "Who are you?" He replied: "Don't you know who I am? Everyday you pray to me. You have a picture of me on our pillow." Then they understood that it was Dr. Sousa Martins. "Do you need anything?" he asked. She replied that she wanted to know if the last body would appear. He replied that it would. The widow asked if it would be possible to recognize him. Sousa Martins replied that the body would be intact, but the face would not be recognizable. Three months later a body was found. Maria Alzira went to see it. She saw that the face had been eaten away, just as Sousa Martins had told them.

The fact that the phenomena of spiritism are not readily dismissed as the traditional superstitions may be one of the reasons for its increasing importance on the local scene.

Another reason may be that the forces of modernization may be manifest in some of the apparitions. Dr. Sousa Martins may possibly be regarded as a spiritual representative of modern medicine, which today is forcefully present on the local scene. The fact that modern politicians and even the Pope appear during the sessions indicates that the forces of modernization indeed are reflected in the spirit beliefs.

It cannot be denied that the forces of modernization are in the process of changing social relations in Nazaré. With these changes, the prebureaucratic beliefs will no doubt finally yield after having served in their way the villagers in Nazaré, helping them to cope with the harsh life and vicissitudes of a fishing community for a long time.

MODERNIZATION AND THE TRANSFORMATION OF BELIEFS

In Nazaré, as elsewhere, the personal interdependence of people is gradually being transformed with the introduction of bureaucratic management of individual needs. This is most strikingly demonstrated in the case of the family Soares. As one of the poorer families of the *praia,* they had suffered many deprivations. The head of the family, Ana, had an unknown number of times consulted with witches, and also with spirit mediums, because of ill health and tribulations of various kinds.

But at the end of the 1970s, her son, who had become an invalid in the war in Angola, had been granted a pension. With several years of back payment, she received a fortune of 400,000 escudos as a lump sum, and every month she received a fairly generous remittance. For the first time in her life, she was without economic worries. She was able to rebuild their modest house and provide it with a color TV and a refrigerator. She was even able to go to the market and buy food she had always wanted, but had never been able to afford.

More important than the material benefits were the changes in her relationships with her neighbors. She no longer feared their envy, which may seem somewhat contradictory. It shows, however, that the fear of envy stings only in a situation of dependency. She no longer needed the material assistance of her network. She told her son that she no longer quarrelled with her former pet enemy, Francelina, and she was on easy terms even with Cara Grande, her former tormentor. The reason she gave for this was that she was no longer afraid of her neighbors because she no longer needed their help. Now the shoe was on the other foot, and she was able to help her relatives with money.

What is most striking, and interesting from our point of view, was that she no longer suffered from *mal d' inveja* (envy), and no longer felt it necessary to consult the witches and spirit media. Her husband, who all his life had suffered from attacks by the devil, also had a new peace of mind and no longer feared the occult forces. He was, however, suffering from more rational fears. He was particularly afraid that someone, driven by envy, would write to the authorities and thus deprive his family of his son's pension.

Although this is merely a single case, it seems to confirm with considerable force that the occult forces of witchcraft, sorcery, and spirit-aggression, which for decades had been afflicting this family, relate to the specific articulation of dependency in a traditional community. With the modernization process in Portugal, now very much in evidence, these traditional beliefs will disappear not merely because of better education, but because of a structural change of the human relationships which sustain the beliefs.

THE URBAN SOCIETY AND THE DISENCHANTED UNIVERSE

In this perspective, Maria Baixinha becomes more than a superstitious little lady. She may be one of the last of her kind, and one of the last who make it possible to observe these age-old beliefs in their authentic setting. One feature of her performance is of particular interest: she does not distinguish between ritual treatment and instrumental, medical treatment. This lack of distinction is characteristic of magic in general.

The distinction was not clearly drawn by the traditional Catholic Church, and was in a restricted sense one of the issues of the Reformation. Although Calvin was not primarily speaking up in the name of reason, his dismissal of the sacraments of

Mother Church paved the way for a new form of rationality. His claim that not the sacraments, but only the will of God can save the soul is more in line with a belief in the independent laws of nature, a belief that would gradually conquer the ground. Not only Descartes, Hume, and related others are responsible for the demise of the enchanted universe, but also the Protestant champions of puritanism. It is not beside the point that the breakthrough of Reformed Protestantism particularly corresponds with the rise of the bourgeoisie as an independent political force.

In this context one may consider that the rise of the bourgeoisie corresponds in some measure to the rise of the modern urban society. The pioneers of bourgeois culture were people who no longer participated in the communal life of the villages. Their transactions and enterprises demanded a detachment from the shackles of close face-to-face human interdependency. Their relationship to the community was to a much greater degree mediated by money and markets, and was to some extent depersonalized by judicial procedures and incipient bureaucratic management. Of the existential realities of this organization of human relationships, a new form of rationality was born.

Protestant puritanism and "reason" as conceived by the Enlightenment appear as two different types of intellectual orientation in the history of ideas. Yet Protestant rationalism, both with regard to the management and to the understanding of religious rituals, has some affinity with the mechanical and disenchanted world view of the Enlightenment, and the two can hardly be regarded as completely unrelated developments. However that may be, the social development from status to contract or from the traditional village to urban society was essential for the decline of the supra-natural explanations of disease and destiny and the triumph of the scientific world view.

The Protestant reformers, in spite of their religious commitment, promoted developments that eventually were to create the secular society that not only spurned magic and superstition, but also increasingly came to regard as superstition the very belief in an almighty God. Given the background of these intellectual developments, the incantations and procedures of Maria Baixinha appear strangely naive. Yet they are true both to the prescientific world view and the ancient beliefs of the Catholic Church that by emphasizing their social precondition, I have called prebureaucratic. Bureaucratic is here used in a wider sense to describe a society in which human relationships are dominated by money, markets, and judicial contracts.

This little woman therefore may be regarded in this sense as an authentic representative of an intellectual tradition that once dominated the European intellectual scene. Just as no clear distinctions were drawn between witchcraft, sorcery and spirit-aggression during the dark centuries of the witch-craze (Henningsen 1980), Maria Baixinha generously distributes her diagnosis among all the different categories of explanation.

Anthropological categories are primarily based upon information from tribal Africa, where the network of social relations is less complex than it was even in the traditional European community. A community where social relations are completely dominated by kinship and tribal affiliation creates corporations that are clearly recognizable, where the distinctions between the different categories of explanations are usually more clearcut.

The lack of a clearcut distinction between sorcery and spirit-aggression among the Nazarenos is consonant with the complexity of the social networks in which ascribed and contractual relations sometimes are part of the same personal dyad, and where each individual for his reputation is dependent upon a faceless, vaguely defined corporation, as for example the *praia*. Although the lack of tidy correlations between various sets of dependencies and types of supra-natural explanations at first glance is frustrating, it corresponds with the complex social reality of Nazaré.

8 / Conclusion

Even a casual observer in Nazaré would be impressed by the communal nature of village life. When walking along the narrow cobblestoned streets, one has to navigate between women and children who have made the street into an extension of the household. A social historian familiar with the writings of Stone (1977), Shorter (1975), Flandrin (1976), and Ariès (1962) would certainly not fail to notice how close to the medieval image of village life contemporary Nazaré seems to be. As we have seen, these first impressions are confirmed by a closer investigation. The significance of the ethnographic realities of present day Nazaré is that its institutions, behavior, and beliefs represent a particularly interesting state in the great transformation of human existence caused by the rise of capitalism and industrial civilization. In the case of Nazaré, however, the problem is not how this local community has been affected by The Great Transformation, but rather how it has not been affected.

Because Nazaré to a certain degree has preserved the communal life of the medieval village, it offers the possibility of studying traditional social forms. By comparing the modern forms with those in Nazaré it is possible to explore the social process of The Great Transformation. Crucial to the communal life in Nazaré is the nature of family life. The crucial event in the modernization of the family is not a change of its composition, but its privatization. As Laslett (1972), among others, has demonstrated, the pre-modern family was not the extended family assumed by Le Play (1877–79). The nuclear family as a residential unit antedates the industrial revolution. The significant change for humans in the modern age was the isolation from kith and kin who in medieval times had more or less free access to the family unit.

In Nazaré a privatization of family life has not taken place. The reason the Nazareno family has not followed the general trend of modernization seems to be female dominance. The families in Nazaré are matrifocal. As is characteristic of matrifocal families in general, the husband's position within the household is marginal, a fact that effectively prevents the kind of matrimonial partnership crucial to privatization.

This fact combines with the local economy and social organization to preserve the communal nature of relationships. A role analysis demonstrates how this fact restricts certain emotional and cognitive developments, and also helps to understand the mental horizon of the traditional village.

As we have seen in the Nazareno case, the communal nature of social life works against the formation of dyadic relationships. The dyadic relationship is essential for the development of self-awareness and consciousness. As G. H. Mead pointed out many years ago (1934), human consciousness reflects the social environment and grows through a process of interaction. The development of the conscious ego seems to follow from a primarily verbal communication with other people. Since human collectives settle for a kind of average articulation of values and norms, the collective inhibits the appreciation of the unsocialized recesses of the human mind that psychoanalysts refer to as the subconscious mind. Because of the sometimes oppressive nature of social norms and values, the hidden and darker side of the human soul is not acknowledged by the conscious ego. This, however, does not pacify the unsocialized part of the soul. In terms of behavior, these darker sides of human nature may manifest themselves in irrational acts and symptoms. Within the framework of a dyadic relationship shielded from the eyes and ears of outsiders, a particular form of trust may under fortunate circumstances develop. It is on this background affective individualism in the family develops. This assures a freedom of expression and relieves the exchanges of the onus of public criticism, censorship, and interference. In the mental climate of an exclusive dyadic relationship, not only forgotten and repressed memories are brought within the grasp of the conscious ego, but repressed desires and motives at odds with social conventions are also brought into a dialogue, and become part of a public, yet strictly circumscribed, sphere of consciousness, the realm of confidence.

Our knowledge of the effects of this particular articulation of relationships derives primarily from psychoanalysis. The kingpin of psychoanalytic therapy is the privileged dyadic relationship established through the method of free associations (Freud 1916). There is nothing in the psychoanalytic process that is not also enacted in the context of everyday life, given that the structure of social relationship allows freedom and confidence. This expansion of consciousness this process facilitates is well-known, although its relevance for our understanding of the psychological aspects of The Great Transformation has not yet been realized.

When human relationships are sustained within the framework of an ever present collective audience, they never reach the same emotional temperature and confidence as in private, dyadic encounters. In a society completely dominated by communal living, the human ego, or self, as described by Marsella, De Vos, and Hsu (1985), will not reach the same degree of individuation.

Under conditions of communal living, the self will not develop its strictly personal and bounded nature, which is the hallmark of the self-conscious ego of men and women in Western industrial civilization—what we may refer to as the modern bourgeois personality. One of the costs of this development is the capacity to feel an awesome loneliness, one of the benefits the luxury of enterprising individualism and personal control.

We know the prebureaucratic European from the reconstructions of the social historians Stone (1977), Shorter (1975), and Flandrin (1976), and also from sociologists like Weber (1904–05) and Elias (1936). Elias has presented the most comprehensive understanding of the development of the modern personality from the medieval simplicity of feudalism to the sophisticated representative of the court society that prepared the ground for the bourgeois mentality. Elias has called his seminal work *Über den Process der Zivilization* (1936) or, *The Civilizing Process*. In colloquial terms, the prebureaucratic personality may be described as more innocent and spontaneous. This prebureaucratic innocence, which should not be confused with benevolence, is the hallmark of a self not yet bounded by privatization.

It is a self without the goffmanesque backstage, a self that primarily knows consciousness as a process of communion and is therefore without the dark secrets of a private life behind the scene. It is a self that has developed as both object and subject merely in a rudimentary way, and therefore is not given to solitary meditation.

The developmental history of the modern, self-conscious ego is the history of privatization and the compartmentalization of life into separate spheres, both in physical and psychological terms. The compartmentalization of life into separate rooms and the disappearance of the teeming livingroom of communal living emerged with the privatization of marriage, affective individualism, and a general process of social differentiation.

This compartmentalization and differentiation spelled the doom of pre-bureaucratic innocence. People no longer slept together in a communal bed. The human body and its natural processes became an object of shame, and a general process of denaturalization started. It is these developments Nobert Elias describes as the civilizing process. It is this process that has not yet run its full course in Nazaré, a fact that provides an opportunity for an observation of the pre-bureaucratic Europeans at a close range.

We have seen that the conjugal pair in Nazaré does not retreat behind the walls of their home to an exclusive privacy. The door remains open to a larger group of kith and kin, and the tie between husband and wife does not develop the same emotional temperature as among the companionate marriages of modern times. Both husband and wife give priority to their respective gender-cultures, and prefer the company of their own age mates to the conjugal relationship. If a woman of the stratum of fishermen tries to follow the bourgeois pattern of a more exclusive pair-bonding, she will be severely criticized, and a man who prefers the company of his wife to that of his age mates is described as *enconado,* trapped by the female sex organ *(cona).*

The dyadic mode of personal relationship is rare among the strata of fishermen. It is not developed within the nuclear family, and is generally absent in peer groups. The mode of social relations is communal, and a close and exclusive dyadic relation between friends is discouraged. In Nazaré three is not a crowd, and attempts to monopolize a relationship will jealously be challenged by the peer group. The establishment of exclusive privacy is next to impossible, and the polarization of social life in a private and a public sphere is only found in a most rudimentary form.

With the communal style of interaction and the lack of compartmentalization of social life in mutually exclusive arenas comes an openness towards the physical nature of human beings. This is most clearly expressed with regard to sexual matters. The Nazarenos do not observe the taboos that the bourgeois culture normally imposes in these matters. Women, more than men, add color to their rhetoric with open references to sexual matters. They see no reason to hide these matters from their children. Ribald sexual jokes are enjoyed by both grown-ups and children in a way that recalls Ariès (1962) descriptions of medieval times. (For example, a woman whose private parts were accidentally exposed by the wind asked a nine-year-old boy present if the sight gave him an erection.)

This Malinowskian attitude toward sex clearly demonstrates that the Nazarenos have retained the medieval attitudes so well described by Focault (1976):

> Sexual practices had little need for secrecy; words were said without undue reticence and things were done without too much concealment, one had a tolerant familiarity with the illicit. Codes regulating the coarse, the obscene, and the indecent were quite lax compared to those of the nineteenth century. It was a time of direct gestures, shameless discourse, and open transgression, when anatomy were shown and intermingled, and knowing children hung about amid the laughter of adults: It was a period where bodies "made a display of themselves." (p. 3)

The same openness is expressed with regard to physical matters in general, demonstrating that the Nazarenos have not taken part in the great process of alienation characteristic of European puritanism. Neither in language nor in behavior do they observe the intellectual distance to human biology expressed by the Puritan conspiracy of silence—its mode of abstraction and control characteristic of what Elias has called the civilizing process. The historical roots of the modern bourgeois personality, then, is partly found in the puritan ideology of Protestantism and the privatization of family life, with its emphasis on the dyadic relationships.

Although the counter-reformation also sent a chill of moralism across Catholic Europe, it failed to domesticate the mind to the same degree as reformed Protestantism. Still left with incense and indulgence, the Catholic Church could purify the sinners and therefore did not demand of the ordinary men and women the sacrifice of extreme puritanic alienation.

The southern and Catholic part of Europe not only preserved its agrarian economy longer, but also to a certain degree the medieval innocence associated with communal living. At the grass roots, at least, life was compartmentalized to a lesser degree, and human beings interacted as whole persons. In terms of role theory, part statuses did not acquire their independence and an intricate role management of the urban style was not demanded. It is to these larger issues that the smaller facts of the everyday life of the Nazarenos speak, demonstrating the singular importance of the structure of relationships.

As we have seen, the universe of the traditional Nazarenos is still enchanted. The forces of communal living and the particular structuring of the relationships in Nazaré is not only operating in the realm of manners, consciousness, and personality, but they also influence the interpretation of destiny. The well-being and health of the Nazarenos are threatened by witch-craft, sorcery, and sometimes by the devil himself. Although they are exposed to the modern world view and have access to the modern medicine, the Nazarenos still stick to their age-old beliefs and keep the local curers busy with spells and magic remedies. Neither knowledge nor information is sufficient to overcome the traditional beliefs, but as one of our cases shows, bureaucratization of subsistence was sufficient to remove the supernatural threats that haunted a family for decades. Although limited to one case, this observation confirms the thesis essential to this presentation: the structure of social relationships is the key to our understanding of the development of manners, personality, and consciousness, as well as of the disenchanted universe.

Glossary

Acumen Ability to judge accurately and perceive clearly.

Affective individualization The restriction of kin ties to close relatives; mate selection based on affection and free choice rather than parental decision.

Alienation A term introduced by Marxist sociologists to describe the breakdown of many-stranded relationships, giving people a feeling of estrangement from society.

Animism Belief that material objects have soul.

Authentic Genuine, unadulterated.

Bacchanal Referring to the Greek god of wine, and usually denoting a wild drinking-party.

Benedictine Referring to the monastic movement of Benedict of Nurcia (480–547). Benedict organized monasteries with *Ora et Labora* (Pray and Work) as the main objective, and changed the attitude toward work as the burden of the slaves to the calling of workers in God's vineyard. Benedictine monasteries prepared the ground for the Protestant work ethic and the breakthrough of industrialism.

Bureaucracy Literally, rule by office. Bureaucrats rule by formalized instructions and derive their influence from delegation by government. Their rule is supposed to be rational and devoid of personal and private interests.

Bureaucratization Organizing social life through bureacracy.

Calvin, John (1509–64) French reformer and champion of an ascetic interpretation of Christianity; regarded by the German sociologist Max Weber as the spiritual architect of capitalism. Calvin advocated an austere life and promoted the Protestant work ethic. Particularly influential in the English-speaking world, although his base of operation was Geneva.

Capitalism An economic system based on a free market where human labor is sold as a market commodity, and economic organizations, like commercial corporations, seek profit in terms of money and rational calculations.

Cognition Knowing and awareness. Derived from the Latin word for thinking, *cogitare* (see *etymology*).

Companionate marriage A marriage where the relationship between husband and wife is more important than their respective relationships to peer groups, wider family ties, and the community. A companionate marriage is expected to be a partnership between equals based on love, affection, and mutual respect.

Deflower The act of taking the maidenhead of a virgin.

Demonology A system of knowledge where misfortunes are explained as the working of evil conspiracies and particularly despised social groups.

Dyadic relationship An exclusive relationship between two people outside the reach of a third person and society at large.

Elopement A custom where prospective partners in a conjugal relationship leave home and consummate a sexual relationship in order to avoid the authority and decisions of their parents.

Emblem A symbolic expression—for example, a heraldic symbol, like the British lion.

Endogamy Marriage inside a defined local group.

Ésprit de corps Spirit of loyalty and friendship that unites members of a group.

Ethos Characteristics of a community or ethnic group. Code of values by which a group or society lives.

Etymology Science of the origin and history of words.

Existential Having to do with the basic questions of human existence, such as life and death, or love and hate.

Exogamy Marriage outside a defined local group.

Extended family A family where married children remain within the territorial, psychological, and economic orbit of their parents. Matrilineally extended families prevail where daughters bring their husbands into the household of their parents. Patrilineally extended families prevail where the sons bring their wives into the household of their family of procreation.

Folk-etymology Ideas of the origin of words based on superficial similarities and deficient knowledge.

Genitor Father in the genetic sense; biological father.

Gesellschaft An urban community where people interact in specialized relationships established through contracts, and where money and markets are more important than non-commercial exchanges.

Gemeinschaft The strongly corporate community in which people are united in many-stranded relationships and non-commercial transactions dominate. Money and markets are of marginal importance. Social ties are inherited (ascribed) rather than established through contact (achieved).

Hierarchy Organization with grades of authority from lowest to highest.

L'ancien régime The regime of the old order. In Europe the term refers to the political order before the French Revolution and the French Enlightenment.

Liminality Characteristic of periods between states of being, as between night and day, or child and grown-up.

Lineage Family line and line of descent.

Manystranded network A situation where human beings are tied to each other in more than one specialized relationship—for example, as neighbors, colleagues, relatives, and friends.

Matriarchal A situation where the society is ruled by women.

Matrifocal A situation where the role of the mother in a conjugal relationship has relevance and respect outside the realm of the house, and where women are equal or sometimes superior to men with regard to social recognition.

Matrilineal A situation where the most important resources in life are transmitted in the female line.

Meritocracy System of leadership by persons of high practical or intellectual ability.

Neolithic revolution The transformation of social life following the establishment of agriculture and sedentary living.

Network The invisible system of ties between human beings.

Occult Hidden for people without extraordinary knowledge; also, in common language, referring to the world of superstition.

Paranoiac Refers to paranoia, a mental condition characterized by irrational fear of persecution.

Pariah Person of no caste or low caste in the Indian caste system; also used to denote social outcasts generally.

Pater Father in the social sense, not necessarily the biological sense.

Patrilineal A situation where the most important resources in life are in the male line, from father to son.

Prebureaucratic Social customs and forms characteristic of societies before the establishment of bureaucracies. Particularly, it refers to the situation in pre-modern Europe.

Privatization of family life A process through which a family group, for example a nuclear family, withdraws from the community into an exclusive realm outside the reach of neighbors and authorities.

Social role A circumscribed complex act expressed in social situations in which behavior relates to social status, that is, rights and duties.

The Great Transformation An expression chosen by the American economist Karl Polanyi to describe the problem of change from agrarian to industrial society.

Tribal Related to tribal organization, i.e., societies based on descent and family. A term that should be substituted by a more neutral term because it is regarded as having colonial overtones.

SOME PORTUGUESE TERMS AND EXPRESSIONS

Aburguesamento Changing lifestyle from that of the fishing community to that of the middle class.

Apoquentada Being harassed by spirits.

A lota The building where the fish auctions are held.

Arte In Nazaré, the term refers to fishing techniques.

Arte xávega Net-fishing from the shore.

Barco de bico Literally, "boat with a beak"; the typical Nazareno boat, with a prow like an inverted beak, sometimes used as the emblem of Nazaré.

Boné The "sixpence" that replaced the traditional cap of Nazareno fishermen.

Bote do alto A large fishing vessel that can navigate the high sea.

Bruxa Witch; also used to denote a curer.

Burgueses People from the middle class. The term corresponds to the French term "bourgeois."

Caldeirada Fish stew, the national dish of Nazaré.

Camarada Comrade, member of the same crew.

Candis Literally "candle boat." Smaller fishing vessel with a lamp to entice the fish.

Carpideira Professional mourner.

Caralho Penis; the favorite exclamation of women in Nazaré.

Casa assombrada Haunted house.

Capitania The port authorities in Nazaré.

Cédula A fisherman's certificate issued by the port authority; a *Capitania*.

Cerola Nazareno underwear with Scottish pattern, used by fishermen.

Comadre Godmother.

Compadre Godfather.

Companheiro Member of a crew.

Corrente Current; in Nazaré it refers to a spiritual power mobilized against attacks from malevolent spirits.

Curandeira Literally, "female curer." In Portuguese folk culture the term refers to a curer who mainly uses incantations and magic in her procedures.

Defumadores The process of driving away evil powers and spirits by smoke.

Ecostado Being the victim of a spirit; literally, "leaning against."

Enconado Literally, "caught by the female sex organ *(cona)*." Refers to a man who neglects the male gender-culture by staying at home with his wife.

Engraixador A smearer of grease, a flatterer; also used to refer to a shoeshine boy.

Enleado Tied by spirits.

Entidades Spirits or small devils of unknown provenance.

Escosês The checkered pattern on Nazareno clothing, presumed to be of Scottish origin.

Éstas casas The house of the witches or *curandeiras* in Nazaré.

Fado Literally, "destiny," but refers also to a particularly nostalgic corpus of songs. Two styles of *fados* prevail, from Lisbon and Coimbra respectively. Coimbra is the old university town in central Portugal.

Fazer os fumadores To drive evil spiritual forces away by smoke—for example, by burning branches from the Palm Sunday procession. The defuming is possibly inspired by the use of incense in church.

Feitiçaria Witchcraft.

Fóquim The wooden rounded boxes traditionally used by the fishermen for their food at sea.

Fulano or Sircano Some average person; an expression corresponding to "Tom, Dick, or Harry."

Gente boa Fishermen's term for respectable people from the middle class.

Gente da praia People belonging to the Nazareno fishing community.

Lancha The smallest fishing vessel of the Nazaré fleet.

Mal d'inveja Various ailments believed to be caused by envy.

Mal olhado Evil eye.

Mestre Generally, chief. Among Nazarenos the term means the skipper of a larger fishing vessel.

Mimoso Spoiled; usually referring to a child.

Muro da censura The wall of blame. A wall along the northern shore of Nazaré where fishermen congregate for gossip, news, and discussions. Also refered to as *Muro da crítica*.

Muro da crítica The wall of criticism.

Muro da vergonna The wall of blame.

Namorada Sweet-heart, girlfriend.

O Inimigo The devil

Paneleiro Literally, "pot-maker." Refers to homosexuals.

Peixeira Female seller of fish.

Pé calçado Feet with shoes. A term used by fishermen to denote members of the middle class.

Pesca à sorte Fishing on the basis of luck. Crew members in Nazaré prefer a share in the catch rather than a fixed salary.

Praia Beach.

Praga A calamity caused by a curse.

Quinhão The parts into which the catch is divided.

Rapa Trawler.

Retornado A Portuguese returned from the colonies lost after the 1974 revolution.

Sol divino A term used in magical incantations; literally, "the divine sun."

Taberna Tavern.

Tal gaijo Literally, "that fellow," meaning the devil.

Ti Uncle or aunt.

Traineira Trawler.

Velho de terra An older fisherman no longer able to go to sea; his job is to mend the nets and serve the crew ashore.

RELIGIOUS REFERENCES

Curação Immacolado de Maria The Immaculate Heart of Virgin Mary.

Dr. Sousa Martins A Portugese folk-Saint. Dr. Sousa Martins was a medical doctor who cared for the needy. He appears frequently in seances in Nazaré.

Nossa Senhora do Carmo The holy Virgin of the Carmelite order established at Mt. Carmel in Palestine in 1155. There are a large number of images of the Virgin in Catholic counties referred to as the Virgin of, for example, Nazaré. *(A Nossa Senhora da Nazaré.)*

Sagrada Curação do Jesus The holy heart of Jesus Christ.

References

Ariès, P. H. 1960. *L'Enfant et la vie familial sous l'ancien régime*. Paris: Plon. (Reprinted as *Centuries of Childhood: A Social History of Family Life*. New York: Vintage, 1962.)

Benedict, R. 1935. *Patterns of Culture*. London: Routledge & Kegan Paul.

Berger, B., and P. L. Berger. 1983. *The War Over the Family*. New York: Anchor Press.

Berger, P. L., and T. Luckman. 1984. *The Social Construction of Reality*. Middlesex, England: Penguin Books.

Brøgger, J. 1971. *Montevarese: A Study of Peasant Society and Culture in Southern Italy*. Oslo: Oslo University Press.

──────. 1986. *Belief and Experience Among the Sidamo: A Case Study Towards an Anthropology of Knowledge*. Oslo: Norwegian University Press.

Burke, P. 1987. *The Historical Anthroplogy of Early Modern Italy*. Cambridge, England: Cambridge University Press.

Douglas, M. 1966. *Purity and Danger*. London: Routledge & Kegan Paul.

Durkheim, E. 1893. *De la division de travail social*. (Reprinted as *The Division of Labor*. New York: Free Press, 1933.)

Elias, N. 1936. *Über den Process der Zivilization*. (Reprinted as *The Civilizing Process*, I and II. New York: Pantheon, 1978.)

Engels, F. 1881. *Der Ursprung der Familie, des Privateigenthums und des Staates*. (Reprinted as *Karl Marx and Fredrich Engels: Selected Works*. New York: International Publisher, 1968.)

Evans-Pritchard, E. E. 1937. *Witchcraft, Oracles and Magic Among the Azande*. Oxford: Clarendon Press.

Flandrin, J. de. 1976. *Families: Parenté, Maison, Sexualité dans l'ancien societé*. (Reprinted as *Families in Former Times*. Cambridge, England: Cambridge University Press, 1979.)

Fonseca, I.M.C. 1979. *Impacto do Mar na Sócio-Economia da Vita da Nazaré*. Manuscript.

Fortune, R. 1932. *Sorcerers of Dobu*. (Reprint, New York: Dutton, 1963.)

Focault, M. 1976. *Histoire de la sexualité: 2.1 La volonté de savoir*. Paris: Gallimard. (Reprinted as *The History of Sexuality*. New York: Pantheon, 1978.)

Fox, R. 1967. *Kinship and Marriage*. Middlesex, England: Penguin.

Freud, S. 1916. *Vorlesungen zu Einführung in die Psychoanalyse*. London: Gesammelte Werke, Imago, 1940–52.

──────. 1930. *Das Unbehagen in der Kultur* London: Gesammelte Werke, 1940–52.

Geertz, C. 1973. *The Interpretation of Cultures*. New York: Basic Books Inc.

Gehlen, A. 1980. *Man in the Age of Technology*. New York: Columbia University Press.

Gilmore, D., and M. M. Gilmore. 1979. *Machismo: A Psychodynamic Approach* (Spain). *Journal of Psychological Anthropology*, vol. 2, 1979, pp. 281–299.

Goffman, E. 1959. *The Presentation of Self in Everyday Life*. New York: Doubleday.

Goody, J. 1983. *The Development of the Family and Marriage in Europe*. Cambridge, England: Cambridge University Press.

Goody, J., J. Thirsk, and P. I. Thompson. 1976. *Family and Inheritance*. Cambridge, England: Cambridge University Press.

Grønnhaug, R. 1969. *Patriarkalsk autoritet og æresideologi i et "peasant"—samfunn i Sør Tyrkia*. Manuscript, Bergen, Norway.

Hannerz, U. 1969. *Soulside: Inquiries into Ghetto Culture and Community*. Stockholm: Almquist & Wiksell.

Henningsen, G. 1980. *The Witches' Advocate: Basque Witchcraft and the Spanish Inquisition*. Reno: University of Nevada Press.

Laslett, P. 1972. *Household and Family in Past Times*. Cambridge, England: Cambridge University Press.

Le Play, P. G. F. 1877–79. *Les Ouvriers Européen: L'organization des Familles*. Tours: 6 vol.

Le Roy Ladurie, E. 1978. *Montaillou: village occitan de 1294 à 1324*. Paris: Gallimard. (Reprinted as *Montaillou: Cathars and Catholics in a French Village, 1294–1324*. London: Scholar Press, 1978.)

Lewis, I. M. 1971. *Ecstatic Religion: An Anthropological Study of Spirit Possession and Animism*. Middlesex, England: Penguin.

Macatrão, S. M. 1988. *Expressoes da orazareth*. Viseu: Edição do Autor.

Malinowski, B. 1929. *The Sexual Life of Savages in Northwestern Melanesia*. London: Routledge & Kegan Paul.

Marsella, A. J., G. de Vos, and F. L. K. Hsu. 1985. *Culture and Self: Asian and Western Perspectives*. New York: Tavistock Publishing.

Mead, G. H. 1934. *Mind, Self and Society*. Chicago: University of Chicago Press.

Mitchell, J. C. 1956. *The Yao Village*. Manchester: Manchester University Press.

Murdock, G. P. 1980. *Theories of Illness: A World Survey*. Pittsburgh, PA: University of Pittsburgh Press.

Paine, R. 1969. *In Search of Friendship*. Man. No. 4 N.S., Vol. 4. No 4, pp. 505–524.

Polanyi, K. 1944. *The Great Transformation*. New York:

Radcliffe-Brown, A. R. 1952. "*Patrilineal and Matrilineal Succession*", in *Structure and Function in Primitive Society*. London: Cohen and West.

Reddy, W. M. 1984. *The Rise of Market Culture*. Cambridge, England: Cambridge University Press.

Said, E. W. 1979. *Orientalism*. New York: Vintage Books.

Schneider, D. and K. Gough (eds). 1961. *Matrilineal Kinship*. Berkeley and Los Angeles: University of California Press.

Shorter, E. 1975. *The Making of the Modern Family*. New York: Basic Books.

Stone, L. 1977. *The Family, Sex and Marriage in England, 1500–1800*. Middlesex, England: Penguin.

Sundt, E. 1850. *Beretning om Fante eller Landstrygerfolket i Norge*. Kristiana S.N.

Tanner, N. 1974. *Matrifocality in Indonesia and Africa and Among Black Americans*. In M. Rosaldo and L. Lamepere (eds), *Women, Culture and Society*. Stanford, CA: Stanford University Press.

Trevor-Roper, H. R. 1970. *The European Witch-craze*. In M. Marwick (ed), *Witchcraft and Society*. Middlesex, England: Penguin.

Tønnies, F. 1887. *Folk Community and Urban-Society*. (Reprinted as *Community and Society*). New York: Harper & Row.

Weber, M. 1904–05. *Die Protestantishe Ethic und der Geist des Kapitalismus, Archiv für Sozialwissenschaft und Sozialpolitik,* Vols. XX and XXI. (Reprinted as *The Protestant Ethic and the Spirit of Capitalism*. New York: Charles Scribner's Sons.)

Wylie, L. 1964. *Village in the Vaucluse; An Account of Life in a French Village*. New York: Harper & Row.